Nelson Science

Starter Level
Teacher's Book

Anthony Russell

OXFORD
UNIVERSITY PRESS

UNIVERSITY PRESS

Great Clarendon Street, Oxford, OX2 6DP, United Kingdom

Oxford University Press is a department of the University of Oxford.

It furthers the University's objective of excellence in research, scholarship, and education by publishing worldwide. Oxford is a registered trade mark of Oxford University Press in the UK and in certain other countries.

First published 2022

British Library Cataloguing in Publication Data

Data available

ISBN: 978-1-382-01762-6
ISBN: 978-1-382-01763-3 (Teacher book only)

1 3 5 7 9 10 8 6 4 2

Paper used in the production of this book is a natural, recyclable product made from wood grown in sustainable forests. The manufacturing process conforms to the environmental regulations of the country of origin.

Printed and bound by CPI Group (UK) Ltd, Croydon, CR0 4YY

Acknowledgements

Cover: Aaron Cushley

Artwork by Q2A Media Services Pvt. Ltd.

Every effort has been made to contact copyright holders of material reproduced in this book. Any omissions will be rectified in subsequent printings if notice is given to the publisher.

Although we have made every effort to trace and contact all copyright holders before publication this has not been possible in all cases. If notified, the publisher will rectify any errors or omissions at the earliest opportunity.

Cover activities

The following activities are based on the Workbook A-C cover images. You can use these stimulus questions according to children's learning to date.

For each of the Workbook cover pictures, ask your learners to look at them carefully.

Workbook A

Ask your learners: what are the children in the picture doing? What games do they play with their friends when they are outside?

Workbook B

Ask your learners to look at the building in the picture. Can they tell you what is on the wall? What are clocks used for? What time do they go for playtime?

Workbook C

The children in the cover image are playing in a park playground. Can your learners name any of the playground equipment (there is a roundabout, a swing and a climbing net)? What is there to play on in their local park?

Contents

Workbook B

Workbook C

How Nelson Science works

LEVEL	PUPIL BOOK	WORKBOOKS	TEACHING SUPPORT	DIGITAL CONTENT ON OXFORD OWL
STARTER LEVEL		Workbook Starter A / Workbook Starter B / Workbook Starter C	Starter Level Teacher's Book	
1	Pupil Book	Workbook	Teacher's Book	
2	Pupil Book	Workbook	Teacher's Book	• digital versions of the *Pupil Books, Workbooks* and *Teacher's Books*
3	Pupil Book	Workbook	Teacher's Book	• assessment support
4	Pupil Book	Workbook	Teacher's Book	• notes for parents and carers
5	Pupil Book	Workbook	Teacher's Book	• curriculum mapping and planning guides
6	Pupil Book	Workbook	Teacher's Book	• vocabulary support

Access the digital content for this course online at
www.oxfordowl.co.uk

Introduction

It is not possible to understand science, nor to work scientifically, without using language and maths. Science develops and grows on the basis of communication – the sharing of questions, ideas and findings – whether in spoken or written form. Language is central to the work of scientists. So, it should not surprise you to find that the contents of the three Nelson Science Starter Level *Workbooks* overlap with those of the Nelson English Starter Level *Workbooks*. Almost every unit in the Nelson English Starter Level *Workbooks* has potential links with science content and approaches.

Naturally **all** the Nelson Science Starter Level *Workbook* activities use language in one or more of its four forms – speaking, listening, reading and writing. At the heart of science is communication, so while 'doing' the science, learners will be using and developing their English language knowledge and skills. It is your role to see these links and overlaps and to make full use of them, achieving the Early Learning Goals in more than one area simultaneously. You should deliberately use the activities in the Nelson Science Starter Level *Workbooks* to teach and develop the language of learners.

The other overlap, though less obvious, is with maths. Science depends on maths. Often the link is hidden by the time the scientific ideas have been accepted and become common knowledge. Counting, measuring, ordering, comparing, finding patterns, shapes and sizes, using estimates and non-standard units, then standard units, using instruments to gather information, recording and sharing information in tables and pictograms, histograms and eventually graphs – how could science operate without these vital mathematical ideas and processes? So, when you put the Nelson Maths Starter Level *Workbooks* alongside the Nelson Science Starter Level *Workbooks* you will find much common ground and again, you will see that many of the Mathematical Early Learning Goals can be achieved through the activities in the Nelson Science Starter Level *Workbooks*. The more you can recognise this potential, the more the activities will reinforce learners' mathematical understanding and skills, while they are learning scientific ideas and skills.

Best practice in classroom management with this age group

As an Early Years educator you are well aware of the vital role of play. It is valuable and important in so many ways and opportunities to incorporate it into language, maths and science activities are numerous and obvious.

The Nelson Science Starter Level *Workbooks* draw on young children's natural curiosity, imagination and physicality. They want – need – to be doing, making, moving, handling, discovering (through independent action and thought) so much about the physical world, which is the stuff of science. It is for you to 'plug into' these natural mental, physical and emotional needs and desires, using them to move learners towards the learning goals across the whole spectrum of content as set out in the English National Curriculum for Years 1 to 6. Let learners play and through that play let them see the world in new ways, with more knowledge and understanding.

You should organise the classroom and outdoor space to provide opportunities to explore, freely and actively. Objects, materials, processes and activities should not be left unchanged for months on end. Novelty – the introduction of the new object and the unknown puzzle – is one way you can maintain learners' curiosity and provide challenges. For instance, displays should be changed often, and new jigsaw puzzles introduced to replace those done many times before.

The whole learning environment should be a rich, stimulating context where learners are able to access materials independently of you and other adults, moving freely about the space. The whole layout and atmosphere should be informal yet set up deliberately by you in a focused way to maximise learners' learning through the various forms of play. Learning and play are not separate, but integrated by your intentional planning, even though learners may not realise your intentions.

Listen and observe a lot so that the room and outdoor space can be matched more closely to learners' interests and levels of understanding. Encourage learners to talk by giving them opportunities to be in class or group conversations as well as with you.

Make use of the daily routine of clearing up – exploit its educational potential and the scientific ideas inherent in it (e.g. sorting, naming, classifying and comparing). Use the element of surprise to grab learners' attention by putting together things normally not seen together (e.g. a soft toy in a display of stones, a carrot in a vase of flowers). Provide problems to be solved such as fitting shapes in holes. Keep the sense of wonder alive through the use of the unfamiliar, the new and the just plain silly (e.g. have a mop or broom with wig, hat and beard standing in the corner).

More guidance is provided below about how to check that learners have understood and how to encourage discussion (see 'Encouraging participation and engagement').

How to use Nelson Science

This *Teacher's Book* is intended to accompany the new updated edition of *Nelson Science*, which has been developed specifically with the needs of international teachers in mind. This new edition provides a complete primary science programme for pupils aged 4 to 11 and their teachers. *Nelson Science* is made up of seven levels (one for each year group). The first level is known as Starter Level and is designed for use in Reception/Foundation levels. The *Nelson Science* course is made up of three Starter Level *Workbooks* (A–C), six *Pupil Books* at later levels, and six corresponding write-in *Workbooks*. All the units are accompanied by comprehensive lesson guidance in the *Teacher's Book*. The *Teacher's Book* contains detailed support for each unit, which will help you to introduce new concepts, and deepen learners' understanding of science.

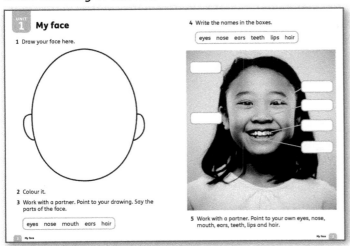

Each unit in the in the *Workbooks* is supported by a corresponding unit in the *Teacher's Book*.

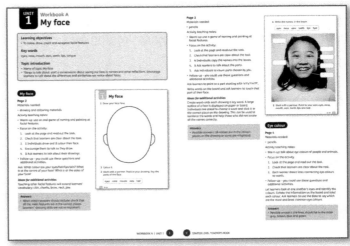

The *Teacher's Book* provides detailed teaching guidance for each unit and answers to the *Workbook* activities.

Read the relevant unit of the *Teacher's Book* before you begin teaching it. It is important to familiarise yourself with the learning objectives, key vocabulary and resources you need before each lesson. The following pages will give you a good understanding of how to use the *Workbooks* and *Teacher's Book* together.

In addition to the printed materials, you can also find lots of supplementary digital resources online on *Oxford Owl*. Please see page xiv for more information.

The *Workbooks*

The contents of the three Nelson Science Starter Level *Workbooks* follow the natural developmental progression of the child. Beginning with themselves in Book A, their personal world of home and school is the focus of Book B and the wider world of the child is looked at in Book C. So, the progression is from the most to the least familiar, drawing on the experience of learners up to this point in their short lives. The intention across all the books is not just to repeat the familiar but to help learners to see it in new ways – scientific ways.

Workbook A - Myself	Workbook B – Home and school	Workbook C – The World around me
• My face	• This is where I live	• Plants
• My body	• This is my school	• Animals
• My family	• Books and pictures	• Weather
• My colours	• Clocks	• Soil
• My clothes	• Time for food	• Buildings
• My toys	• Time for school	• Shops
• My shadow	• Playtime	• Museums
• My voice	• Time for sleep	• In the street
• My feelings	• Special days	• In the park
• My health	• Growing	• Staying safe
• My pets	• Changes	• Holidays

The format of the *Workbooks* is maintained throughout. This helps you and the learners to become familiar with how they 'work' and reduces the time needed to settle down to the tasks.

Each unit has four activities and each of these activities fills one page of the *Workbook*. Overall, the *Workbooks* each have 44–45 pages of tasks for the children, with plenty of blank space provided for them to draw, copy and write their answers. Whatever they put in those spaces should be seen by you as the 'outcomes' of the tasks and it should form the basis of conversations between yourself and the individual learners, plus a stimulus to group interactions. Filling the blanks, answering the questions, completing the tasks – these are not the end you have in mind. They are merely the 'jumping-off point' for the development of learners' scientific knowledge, understanding and skills. Make good use of learners' recorded responses.

Science is a 'body of knowledge': it includes vast amounts of facts, information, ideas, concepts and explanations, but science is also an approach – a way, a method, a set of processes. It is by using these process 'skills' that science is able to collect the reliable evidence needed to 'prove' an idea and establish the facts. On every page the *Workbooks* provide opportunities to apply and develop these skills. These are as important as any scientific knowledge that can be learned through the tasks.

The skills of working scientifically

Encouraging participation and engagement

Set out below is a list of the skills included in the Workbook tasks.

- **Talking** – this is listed first for two reasons. It is the most frequent skill used in the tasks and for Early Years children it is the most important form of language they have and it will form the basis of their other language skills, so it comes at the top of the list. Encourage learners to talk as they do the tasks and then to talk about what they have done. They will reveal so much of what they know and understand as they talk and this will be invaluable for you to help them develop their scientific ideas. Talking is one form of reporting. Showing their drawings and their models is another. Scientists are expected to report results and to take part in the discussions which they provoke. You can help learners to develop this habit by using the familiar 'show and tell' approach to the tasks in the *Workbooks*.

- **Observing** – this is the fundamental process of all science. It is not named this way in the *Workbooks*. The more familiar words 'look', 'feel' and 'listen' are used. These are all forms of observation and numerous tasks involve one or more opportunities to use them.

- **Measuring** – this is a special form of observation and at this age 'formal' measures are largely not appropriate. However, *time* is the focus of one unit and it uses learners' familiarity with 'minutes', 'hours' and the notion of these units being of different 'sizes'. Build on this. In other units there are opportunities to compare sizes of various kinds and comparing leads towards the use of units of measurement suited to the property being compared (e.g. length, mass). The language needed for this notion of 'sizes' is of general importance, not just in science; 'longer', 'shortest', 'heaviest', 'taller', 'light', etc. The Maths Early Learning Goals include the use of comparatives, so here is a good example of the two subject areas overlapping and supporting one another.

- **Recording** – science has developed through building up vast records of what has been observed over centuries. This habit of observing followed by recording needs to be taught from the start and the tasks in the *Workbooks* give learners plenty of chances to do this. The word 'record' is not used but 'draw' and 'write' are used in the majority of tasks.

- **Drawing** – the place of drawing in science is important, both as a way of capturing the appearance of objects – recording them – and in the creation of diagrams that express relationships and processes. This important skill matches well with the natural inclination of young children to 'make marks' of one kind or another, especially if provided with the means – crayons, paints, pencils, etc. Over time learners will develop better hand–eye coordination and motor skills will improve with practice. The result will be a closer and closer representation of 'reality' in their drawings. In the Early Years we accept learners' attempts, regardless of the lack of accuracy or detail. So, drawing a picture may seem far from science, but actually it is central; it involves looking (observation) and recording. It is a creative process in which the learner's mind processes what is being observed and attempts to express the information using line, shape and colour. There is an obvious overlap with the 'Expressive arts and design' Early Learning Goals.

- **Writing** – at the Early Years stage, much of the writing will be copying words from the printed page. The writing of numerals is another common part of an activity – another form of recording, following a counting task. Some tasks ask learners to write their own words and you will often provide what they need, but letting them 'do their best' is an important stage in developing their writing skills.

- **Comparing** – (see measuring above).

- **Sorting** – even young children have lots of experience of this, one of the fundamental process skills of science. Putting things into groups and sets is the foundation of classification, used across all the sciences. When you ask learners to tidy things away you are giving them opportunities to practise their sorting skills. The criteria you set will vary – colour, shape, size, material, etc. – but all such sorting is worthwhile, especially if you question learners about how they are doing it. Science depends on noting similarities and differences and using these to classify the natural world – the plants, the animals, the elements, the rocks, the clouds, etc. Tidying the room can feed into this most vital of scientific skills. Many tasks in the *Workbooks* ask learners to identify things that belong together – to match, to pair, to separate, to group. Ask learners to tell you why they sort things as they do. Their answers will reveal what criteria they are using in their minds to do the task. Through challenging their ideas you can provoke them into reconsidering their way of seeing things – offering the chance for learning.

- **Naming or identifying** – science has so many special words and it uses common words in special ways too. Naming is its way of fixing identities so that discussion and sharing can proceed smoothly. All your learners have names, as do their families and friends, so the idea of a name is familiar. In science this notion is extended across every thing and every process in the universe – nothing is left un named. Very little 'formal' scientific naming is expected at this stage, but the idea of naming things is the basic idea to be taught and learned. The tasks in the *Workbooks* make use of the names already known by learners and set out to extend their vocabulary too. You will be the source of many of these new names, but learners should be encouraged to share what they know; children differ in their life experiences, so some will know things others do not. Draw on this knowledge. The identification and naming of numerals is part of many tasks in the *Workbooks* and is part of the Maths Early Learning Goals.

- **Ordering** – this is a particular form of sorting, where one feature or characteristic is used to arrange items in a sequence of some kind. Observation, comparing and sorting are all part of this process and it becomes a more important skill as learners' science develops. Tasks in the *Workbooks* give opportunities for this skill to be used.

- **Finding patterns** – this is crucial to our understanding of the natural world. Patterns 'tell us something'. Often, they reveal a relationship between two or more processes, events or objects. Great advances in science have been made because someone noticed a pattern in observations. Our understanding has been deepened and our grasp of the complexity of the universe has strengthened. Tasks involving patterns are included in the *Workbooks* and even when the 'content' of the pattern is not particularly 'scientific', the process is still contributing to learners' science skills.

- **Predicting** - on the basis of patterns we are able to make predictions which we can test, thus clarifying our ideas and ruling out other possibilities. You can use the tasks in the *Workbooks* to ask learners to say 'what would happen if' and 'what could happen next'; these open-ended questions give them the chances to speculate and use their present knowledge and understanding to answer you. Of course, imagination will be involved; science grows out of imagination. It is a very creative human activity, built on asking questions and 'dreaming up' ways to answer them. Again, the Early Learning Goals for the 'Expressive arts and design' are linked to this aspect of science.

Workbook topics and the English National Curriculum Year 1 to Year 6

The *Workbooks* are intended to introduce the science curriculum for Years 1 to 6. The *Workbooks* include all the topics in the curriculum except for five (Earth and beyond, magnets, evolution, rocks and states of matter.) All the *Workbook* topics will be extended and developed as learners move through their primary years. In that sense, the time spent on the Early Years tasks acts as an investment in learners' science education. They are not just time-filling activities – they are steps on the way to the learning objectives outlined in the English National Curriculum.

Some topics, such as plants and materials, occur more frequently. All of them are introduced in ways suited to the age of your learners. Some tasks depend on adult support, but most are for learners to do independently.

Using the Teacher's Book

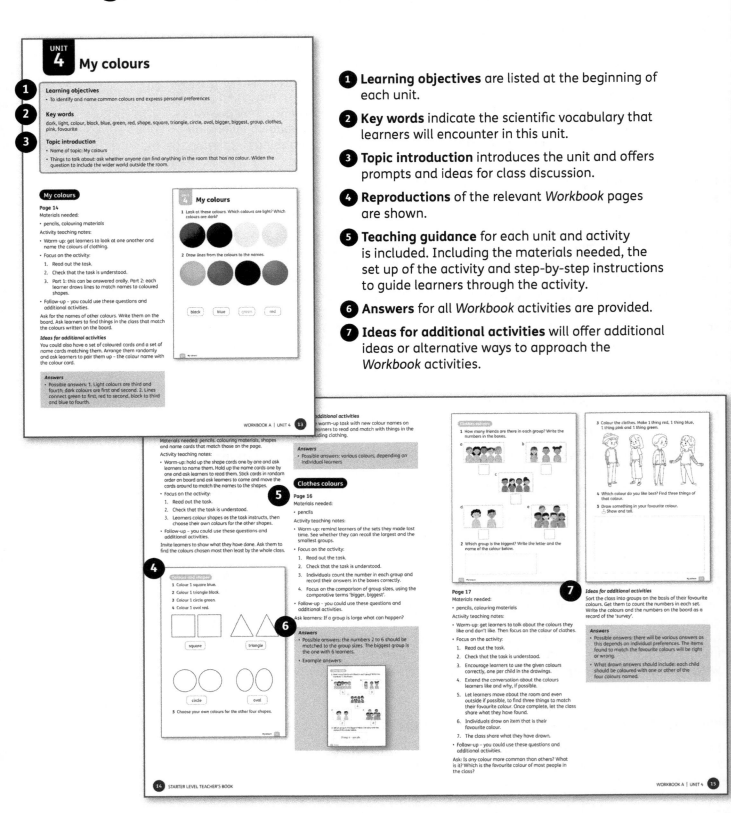

1 **Learning objectives** are listed at the beginning of each unit.

2 **Key words** indicate the scientific vocabulary that learners will encounter in this unit.

3 **Topic introduction** introduces the unit and offers prompts and ideas for class discussion.

4 **Reproductions** of the relevant *Workbook* pages are shown.

5 **Teaching guidance** for each unit and activity is included. Including the materials needed, the set up of the activity and step-by-step instructions to guide learners through the activity.

6 **Answers** for all *Workbook* activities are provided.

7 **Ideas for additional activities** will offer additional ideas or alternative ways to approach the *Workbook* activities.

Using the Workbooks

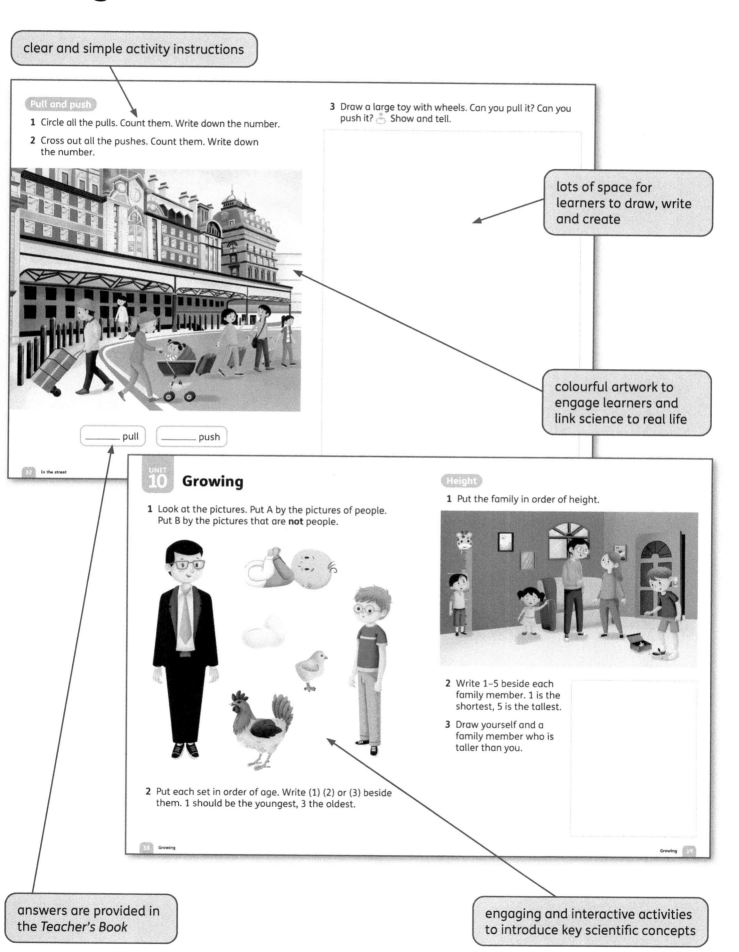

clear and simple activity instructions

Pull and push

1 Circle all the pulls. Count them. Write down the number.

2 Cross out all the pushes. Count them. Write down the number.

3 Draw a large toy with wheels. Can you pull it? Can you push it? Show and tell.

lots of space for learners to draw, write and create

colourful artwork to engage learners and link science to real life

_____ pull   _____ push

UNIT 10 Growing

1 Look at the pictures. Put A by the pictures of people. Put B by the pictures that are **not** people.

2 Put each set in order of age. Write (1) (2) or (3) beside them. 1 should be the youngest, 3 the oldest.

Height

1 Put the family in order of height.

2 Write 1–5 beside each family member. 1 is the shortest, 5 is the tallest.

3 Draw yourself and a family member who is taller than you.

answers are provided in the _Teacher's Book_

engaging and interactive activities to introduce key scientific concepts

Using the digital content

This edition of *Nelson Science* is supported by additional digital resources available online on **Oxford Owl**. These include:

- digital versions of the *Workbooks* and *Teacher's Book* to support planning and for front of class display
- a set of printable assessments with a progress tracking tool and mark scheme
- guidance for you to share with children's parents or carers about their child's learning, including support for homework and ideas for incorporating science into everyday life
- vocabulary support
- curriculum correlation charts
- support for your planning.

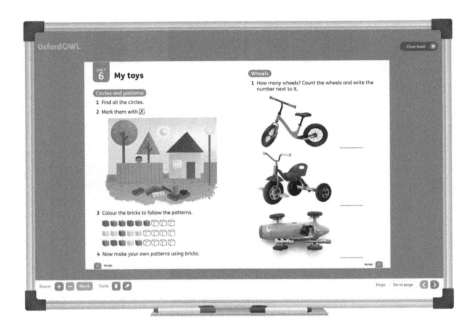

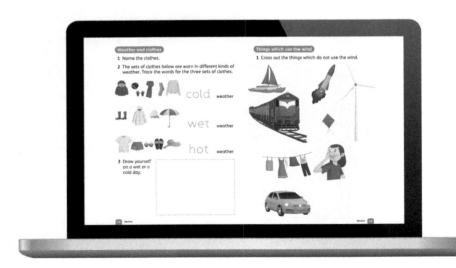

Scope and sequence

Use these tables to support your planning. We recommend teaching units in this order, as the progression of units is designed to support learners in building their skills and knowledge and making connections across the different strands.

Scientific skills

Ideas and evidence
- try to answer simple questions by collecting evidence through observation

Plan investigative work
- make **predictions**, asking 'what would happen if?' and 'what could happen next?'

Obtain and present evidence
- measure time and size in order to collect evidence
- order, compare and sort simple data
- record data through drawing and writing

Consider evidence and approach
- observe patterns through 'look', 'feel' and 'listening'
- name simple scientific words
- classify similar things into groups (e.g. rocks and plants)

Workbook A

Unit	Unit title	Learning objectives	Key words
1	My face	• To name, draw, count and recognise facial features	eyes, nose, mouth, ears, teeth, lips, tongue
2	My body	• To name, recognise, draw, measure and compare parts of the body	leg, arm, foot, hand, finger, toe, neck, belly button, hand span, foot size, weight, height, measure
3	My family	• To compare family members and identify how their ages are related to what they are able to do	family, sister, brother, younger, older, adult, children, baby, youngest, oldest, talk, walk, read, draw, feed, toilet
4	My colours	• To identify and name common colours and express personal preferences	dark, light, colour, black, blue, green, red, shape, square, triangle, circle, oval, bigger, biggest, group, clothes, pink, favourite
5	My clothes	• To name and compare items of clothing and relate them to their uses	pair, count, clothes, wear, feet, same, different, order, size, smallest, biggest, decorate
6	My toys	• To recognise and continue patterns • To compare a variety of toys • To sort items that are used together	toys, circles, bricks, pattern, pair, favourite, wheels
7	My shadow	• To explore and learn more about shadow formation and behaviour • To identify the link between the sun's light and shadow formation	shadow, shape, sun, lose, play, game
8	My voice	• To be more aware of levels of sound • To be able to use their voices in a variety of ways	voice, sing, talk, shout, whisper, message, mouth, sounds, animal
9	My feelings	• To identify and describe various feelings	feelings, face, sad, happy, angry, excited, tired, afraid, name, show
10	My health	• To understand some of the ways they can protect their health • To know that diet and exercise are important for good health	health, teeth, clean, wash, dry, run, swim, jump, climb, ride, meal, foods, eat
11	My pets	• To recognise and name the different ways pets move • To identify and name various common pets • To understand that foods and homes must be matched to pets	pets, legs, count, cat, dog, fish, tortoise, parrot, rabbit, canary, foods, order, size, move, swim, fly, walk, run, hop, home

Workbook B

Unit	Unit title	Learning objectives	Key words
1	This is where I live	• To identify, name and match rooms and their contents, identifying some characteristics	live, home, room, kitchen, bathroom, bedroom, living room, circle, round, soft, hard
2	This is my school	• To identify and name various activities • To sort items on the basis of colour	school, girls, boys, uniform, blue, green, brown, play, game, like, dislike, best, most
3	Books and pictures	• To match numbers and objects • To name and draw fruits and animals • To make a simple book with pictures	book, make, fruit, animal, draw, alphabet, page, read, number, banana, stone, leaves, bean, choose
4	Clocks	• To know the order and position of the numerals on a clock face • To pair the two forms of clock times and to count minutes • To match activities to the times of the day	clock, number, time, pair, hands, minutes, underline
5	Time for food	• To identify, name and draw common fruits and vegetables and other foods • To sort and count sets of kitchen items • To identify dangers in the kitchen	food, home, banana, orange, lemon, fruit, cut, share, count, plates, yellow, bowl, blue, tumbler, knives, red, green, danger, plant
6	Time for school	• To complete the names of animals and plants • To measure using squared paper • To compare lengths and put things in order of length and size • To sort and count flowers and leaves	letter, measure, square, count, longest, shape, order, size, smallest, leaves, flowers, colour, set
7	Playtime	• To use blocks to make various shapes • To identify various activities, including forms of movement • To make a windmill	shape, block, animal, windmill, run, play, walk, swim, fly, slide, hop, run
8	Time for sleep	• To name objects and identify their textures • To sort objects related to sleep • To describe stories and dreams	sleep, feel, name, story, bedtime, favourite, dream, cross out
9	Special days	• To identify and name objects • To sort items • To describe events and experiences • To identify movements and activities • To identify and continue patterns	special, wedding, party, birthday, cross out, procession, carnival, flags, costume, moving, pattern, order, size, line, number, playing, dancing, clapping, singing, smiling
10	Growing	• To put human life stages in order • To identify changes in their bodies and skills • To investigate bean germination and growth	set, order, age, bean, grow, measure, first, last, ride
11	Changes	• To identify pulls and pushes • To identify the stages in a bird's life • To be able to sow seeds and know what they need to germinate	class, pull, push, story, bird, adult, eggs, finish, make up, seed, soil, water, plant, leaves

Workbook C

Unit	Unit title	Learning objectives	Key words
1	Plants	• To arrange items in order of size • To know that leaves, seeds, flowers and fruits vary in size, shape and colour • To identify and name seeds, flowers and fruits	plant, leaf, collect, order, size, seed, pea, bean, cashew, sunflower, rice, count, red, blue, yellow, flower, shape, fruit, orange, banana, strawberry, melon, apple, mango, tomato
2	Animals	• To identify and name some animals • To know that each animal fits its environment • To identify animal movements • To complete animal drawings	animal, adult, young, bird, count, dog, cat, sheep, horse, penguin, hen, legs, walk, swim, fly, slide, move, desert, Arctic, jungle, sea, grassland, place
3	Weather	• To identify and name some weather elements • To know that the weather affects what we wear • To identify various weather conditions • To know that we use the wind in various ways • To understand that rain and snow return water to the streams, rivers, etc.	weather, lightning, cloud, sun, hail, snow, wind, rain, wet, hot, cold, clothes, cross out, fan, move, drop, pond, stream, river, lake, sea, snowy, mountain, glacier, ice cap, iceberg
4	Soil	• To know that some living things live in the soil • To know that we eat some roots • To know that seeds need certain things to grow	soil, animal, underground, cross out, touch, home, roots, eat, plant, sweet potato, carrot, radish, beetroot, seed
5	Buildings	• To be able to identify and continue patterns • To identify and name building types	building, wall, pattern, block
6	Shops	• To identify and name fruits and vegetables • To sort containers into sets • To sort and name sea-foods • To identify and name materials used to make furniture • To describe and name textures	shop, fruit, vegetable, underline, count, favourite, circle, jar, set, can, tin, fish, shell, leg, furniture, feel, soft, rough, hard, smooth, fabric
7	Museums	• To sort and identify musical instruments on the basis of how they are played • To identify animal, plant and non-living things • To identify and name materials • To be able to make a pot from clay	museum, hit, circle, blow, shake, pluck, beads, seeds, can, pot, stone, metal, wood, fabric, clay, pattern
8	In the street	• To sort things on the basis of their movements or sounds • To identify pushes and pulls and to use them	street, sort, set, engine, animal, person, moving, sounds, circle, number, cross out, machine, pull, push, wheels
9	In the park	• To be able to identify up and down • To be able to slide things down a slope • To arrange things in order of height • To identify and name plant parts • To make a bark wax rubbing • To make shapes that roll • To identify floating items • To identify and name various forms of movement	park, up, down, slide, number, order, height, shorter, taller, tree, bark, leaf, bud, twig, wax, rubbing, lake, slope, roll, shape, float, tick, circle, movement, dough, plasticine
10	Staying safe	• To identify and name safety features in the street and the classroom • To identify and name sockets, switches and plugs • To know that electricity is used by many appliances • To identify and name dangers, including electricity and flames	safe, symbol, tick, count, crossing, match, traffic, lights, electricity, circle, socket, plug, number, flame, safety, dangerous, danger
11	Holidays	• To identify and name various forms of transport • To mime transport movements	holiday, match, train, car, boat, plane, bus, tick, circle, mime, movement

Workbook A
My face

Learning objectives

- To name, draw, count and recognise facial features

Key words

eyes, nose, mouth, ears, teeth, lips, tongue

Topic introduction

- Name of topic: My face
- Things to talk about: start a conversation about seeing our face in mirrors and other reflections. Encourage learners to talk about the differences and similarities we notice about faces.

My face

Page 2

Materials needed:

- drawing and colouring materials

Activity teaching notes:

- Warm-up: use an oral game of naming and pointing at facial features.
- Focus on the activity:
  1. Look at the page and read out the task.
  2. Check that learners are clear about the task.
  3. **1** Individuals draw and **2** colour their face.
  4. Encourage them to talk as they draw.
  5. **3** Ask learners to talk about their drawings.
- Follow-up – you could use these questions and additional activities.

Ask: What colour are your eyes/hair/lips/skin? What is at the centre of your face? What is at the sides of your face?

Ideas for additional activities

Touching other facial features will extend learners' vocabulary: chin, cheeks, brow, neck, jaw.

Answers

- What drawn answers should include: check that all the main features are in the correct places. Learners' drawing skills are not so important.

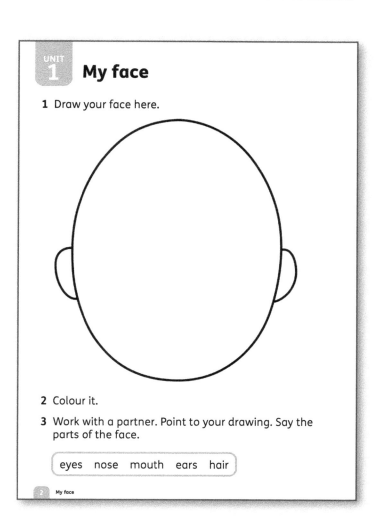

UNIT 1 My face

1 Draw your face here.

2 Colour it.

3 Work with a partner. Point to your drawing. Say the parts of the face.

eyes   nose   mouth   ears   hair

2   My face

Page 3

Materials needed:

• pencils

Activity teaching notes:

• Warm-up: use a game of naming and pointing at facial features.

• Focus on the activity:

1. Look at the page and read out the task.

2. Check that learners are clear about the task.

3. **4** Individuals copy the names into the boxes.

4. **5** Ask learners to talk about the parts.

5. Ask individuals to count parts chosen by you.

• Follow-up – you could use these questions and additional activities.

Ask learners to point to a part starting with 'n'/'e'/'m'/'l'.

Write words on the board and ask learners to touch that part of their face.

Ideas for additional activities

Create word cards each showing a key word. A large outline of a face is displayed on paper or board. Individuals are asked to choose a word and stick it in the correct place on the drawing. This can be used to reinforce the words and help those who did not locate all the names correctly.

Answers

• Possible answers: all names are in the correct places on the drawing *or* some are misplaced.

4 Write the names in the boxes.

eyes   nose   ears   teeth   lips   hair

5 Work with a partner. Point to your own eyes, nose, mouth, ears, teeth, lips and hair.

My face 3

Eye colour

Page 4

Materials needed:

• pencils

Activity teaching notes:

• Warm-up: talk about eye colours of people and animals.

• Focus on the activity:

1. Look at the page and read out the task.

2. Check that learners are clear about the task.

3. Each learner draws lines connecting eye colours to words.

• Follow-up – you could use these questions and additional activities.

Let learners look at one another's eyes and identify the colours. Collate the information on the board and total each colour. Ask learners to use the data to say which are the most and least common eye colours.

Answers

• Possible answers: the lines should be in the order grey, brown, blue and green.

Eye colour

1 Draw lines from the eyes to the colours.

green

grey

brown

blue

Our faces

1 Draw the missing parts of the face.

2 Colour the drawing. Name the parts of the face.
Show and tell.

Our faces

Page 5

Materials needed:

• drawing and colouring materials

Activity teaching notes:

• Warm-up: talk about the parts of the face that are in pairs and those that are not.

• Focus on the activity:

1. Look at the page and read out the task.

2. Check that learners are clear about the task.

3. **1** Individuals draw the missing part of the face, trying to match up the positions and sizes of the paired features.

4. **2** Learners colour their drawings.

5. Encourage learners to talk as they draw.

• Follow-up – you could use these questions and additional activities.

Ask learners to display their drawings for the class to see. Let them talk about the drawings.

Answers

• What drawn answers should include: the missing features of the face should be located roughly in the correct places.

Learning objectives

• To name, recognise, draw, measure and compare parts of the body

Key words

leg, arm, foot, hand, finger, toe, neck, belly button, hand span, foot size, weight, height, measure

Topic introduction

• Name of topic: My body

• Things to talk about: start a conversation about the variety of parts the body has and the many things we can use them. Encourage learners to name some body parts.

My body

Page 6

Materials needed:

• pencils

Activity teaching notes:

• Warm-up: call out names of body parts and learners respond by touching the named parts.

• Focus on the activity:

1. Read out the task.

2. Check that learners understand the task.

3. **1** Learners count each of the body parts listed.

4. **2** Learners record the numbers in the table.

5. **3** Learners talk about the body parts they have counted.

• Follow-up – you could use these questions and additional activities.

Ask learners to name some of the ways they use the body parts (e.g. hands for eating, drawing; feet for walking, kicking balls).

Ideas for additional activities

Ask individuals to demonstrate using one hand or two, or one foot or two to perform some action (e.g. opening a pot with a lid, riding a scooter or tricycle, climbing).

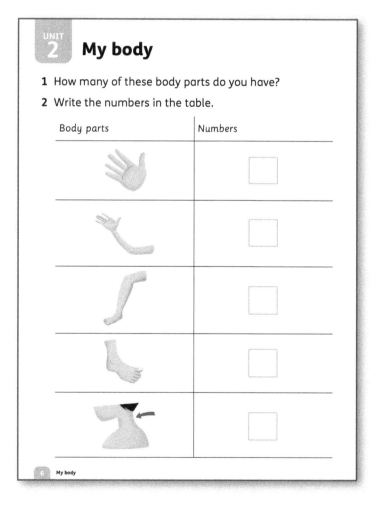

- Possible answers: the numbers of each part are correctly recorded *or* not.
- Example answers:

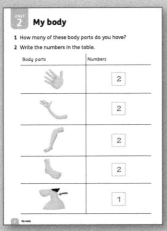

Our hands

Page 7

Materials needed:

- pencils

Activity teaching notes:

- Warm-up: ask learners to perform actions with their hands (e.g. make a fist, point at things, spread their fingers as far as possible, clap).
- Focus on the activity:
  1. Read out the task.
  2. Check that learners understand the task.
  3. **1** Individuals draw round their hand.
  4. **2** Individuals copy the text: This is my **hand**.
  5. **3** Individuals write 'F' on a finger.
- Follow-up – you could use these questions and additional activities.

Ask learners show their drawings to the class.

Ask individuals to hold up their thumbs and touch the thumb in their drawing.

Ideas for additional activities

Ask learners to explore what the thumb can do and other fingers cannot do: it can touch each of the other fingers one by one. This is a very useful action, making the human hand very flexible and useful in making things.

- Possible answers: 'F' is put in the correct position on the drawings. Text has been copied correctly in the right places.
- Example answers:

- What drawn answers should include: the outline clearly shows shapes of fingers.

> **Our hands**
>
> **1** Draw around your hand.
>
> **2** Fill in the missing word:
>
> This is my _____
>
> **3** Look at your drawing. Write F on a finger.
>
> My body   7

Measuring

Page 8

Materials needed:

- pencils, word cards (hand size, foot size), interlocking blocks

Activity teaching notes:

- Warm-up: have 'hand' and 'foot size' on word cards and display them.

- Focus on the activity:

  1. Read out the task.

  2. Check that learners understand it.

  3. Explain how the task will be organised.

  4. When the measures are done, ask the question about the length of the hand and the foot. Compare them and answer the question about which is the longer.

  5. Encourage learners to talk about the measurements freely, expressing their own points of interest and ideas.

- Follow-up – you could use these questions and additional activities.

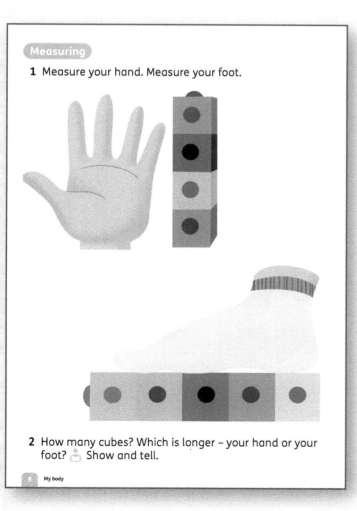

Measuring

1 Measure your hand. Measure your foot.

2 How many cubes? Which is longer – your hand or your foot? Show and tell.

8 My body

Ask learners to share their two measures with the class and collate them on the board. Ask learners to find the longest foot and the longest hand. Does the longest foot belong to the person with the longest hand? Ask the same about the shortest. Make frequent use of the comparatives 'longest', 'shortest', 'longer', 'shorter'.

Ideas for additional activities

Invite learners to make other measurements of individual fingers and compare them.

> **Answers**
> - Possible answers: the figures should be entered in the correct places in the table.
> - Example answers: hand = 4 blocks high; foot = 5 blocks long

Body parts

Page 9

Materials needed:

- pencils

Activity teaching notes:

- Warm-up: ask learners to touch named body parts that are included in the activity. Correct answers that mis-identify parts.

- Focus on the activity:

  1. Read out the task.

  2. Check that learners understand it.

  3. Read the sentences aloud one by one and give learners time to decide whether or not to cross them out.

  4. Individual learners cross out the sentences they think are wrong.

  5. Sing or teach the song about body parts.

- Follow-up – you could use these questions and additional activities.

Invite learners to show body parts that can bend (jointed). Challenge them to find as many as possible, not just those in the activity on this page.

Ideas for additional activities

Use an outline drawing of a child for learners to add key word cards to it in the right places for the body parts.

Put the cards in the wrong places and ask learners to correct them.

> **Answers**
> - Possible answers: crossed-out sentences should be: **a), c), e)**.

Body parts

1 Draw lines from the names to the body parts.

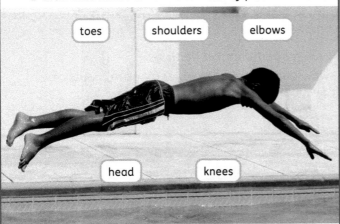

toes shoulders elbows

head knees

2 Cross out the sentences that are wrong:

a) The shoulders are at the bottom of the body.

b) The shoulders are at the top of the body.

c) The elbows are at the top of the arms.

d) The elbows are in the middle of the arms.

e) The knees are at the top of the legs.

f) The knees are in the middle of the legs.

3 Sing the song 'Head, shoulders, knees and toes' and touch the body parts when you say their names.

My body   9

UNIT 3 My family

My family

Page 10

Materials needed:

- pencils

Activity teaching notes:

- Warm-up: talk about adults' and children's roles, and how they differ.

- Focus on the activity:

  1. Read out the task.

  2. Check that the task is understood.

  3. Allow learners to talk about the picture in pairs, then share comments with the class.

  4. Ask individuals to compare the picture with their own families and say whether it is different or the same. Ask them to explain any differences.

  5. The counting should be done individually. Numbers should be written in the spaces.

- Follow-up – you could use these questions and additional activities.

Ask learners to copy the terms 'adults' and 'children'.

Ideas for additional activities

Encourage discussion about the differences in the families of children in the class. This will widen their understanding of family relationships, beyond their own experience.

> **Answers**
> - Possible answers: adults – 4; children – 4

UNIT 3 **My family**

1 Look at the picture.

2 What is the same as your family? What is different?

3 Count the adults. Count the children.

There are _____ adults.

There are _____ children.

10 My family

Young and old

Page 11

Materials needed:

• pencils

Activity teaching notes:

• Warm-up: start a conversation about what learners are looking forward to being able to do as they get older.

• Focus on the activity:

 1. Read out the task.

 2. Check that the task is understood.

 3. Individuals put X on all the things they think the baby cannot do.

 4. Learners discuss in pairs what they think. Ask individuals to explain their answers. How do they know? What evidence do they have?

• Follow-up – you could use these questions and additional activities.

Invite learners to try to work out why the baby is not able to do all the things they can do and tell their ideas to the class.

Ideas for additional activities

Ask learners to put the baby's learning in order – what they will be able to do first, next, later, etc. Pay particular attention to the last thing in the list. Ask learners to give reasons for their answers.

> **Answers**
> • Possible answers: X should be put on talk, walk, read, use toilet, feed itself.

Page 12

Materials needed:

• pencils

Activity teaching notes:

• Warm-up: start a conversation about birthdays and sort the class in order, getting them to stand or sit in a line from oldest to youngest.

• Focus on the activity:

 1. Read out the task.

 2. Check that the task is understood.

 3. Give learners time to look closely at the picture and to ask you questions to clarify what they see.

 4. Individuals write the numbers 1 to 7 in the boxes under the people in the picture.

 5. Let learners share their answers with one another then bring the class together and compare what they have written.

 6. Talk about similarities and differences in learners' answers.

• Follow-up – you could use these questions and additional activities.

Ask: What changes a lot between stages 1 and 2?

Ideas for additional activities

Give learners sheets of paper for them to draw an adult doing something children cannot do.

> **Answers**
> • Possible answers: the order should be: 1: baby, 2: pre-school child, 3: school age child, 4: teenager, 5: adult man, 6/7: grandmother *or* grandfather. The order of the pairs of adults is not important, just that the grandparents should be the last.

3 Look at the drawings.

3

2

4 Number them in order from the youngest to the oldest. Write 1 for the youngest and 7 for the oldest.

5 Discuss this with a partner. Do you agree?

In my family

Page 13

Materials needed:

- pencils, colouring materials

Activity teaching notes:

- Warm-up: remind learners about filling the space on the page with their drawing.

- Focus on the activity:

   1. Read out the task.

   2. Check that the task is understood.

   3. Encourage learners to talk as they draw, identifying and naming family members.

   4. The counting task is simple but individuals may need help in using the numerals to record their answers. The comparatives – older/younger are useful terms for learners to know and use.

- Follow-up – you could use these questions and additional activities.

Ask: If you have no brothers or sisters, would you like to have one? Which would you choose?

Can you name something your older sister/brother can do that you cannot do?

Ideas for additional activities

Invite learners to add the ages of and/or order the children shown in the drawing.

Answers
- Possible answers: numbers will depend on family sizes.
- What drawn answers should include: drawings will vary enormously, both in skill level and the number of people shown. Check that individuals have included themselves in the drawing.

In my family

1 Draw your family. Show and tell.

2 How many people are in your family? Fill in the boxes.

My family has ☐ *people.*

I have ☐ *sisters.* ☐ *Older than me.* ☐ *Younger than me.*

I have ☐ *brothers.* ☐ *Older than me.* ☐ *Younger than me.*

My family   13

My colours

Learning objectives

• To identify and name common colours and express personal preferences

Key words

dark, light, colour, black, blue, green, red, shape, square, triangle, circle, oval, bigger, biggest, group, clothes, pink, favourite

Topic introduction

• Name of topic: My colours

• Things to talk about: ask whether anyone can find anything in the room that has no colour. Widen the question to include the wider world outside the room.

My colours

Page 14

Materials needed:

• pencils, colouring materials

Activity teaching notes:

• Warm-up: get learners to look at one another and name the colours of clothing.

• Focus on the activity:

 1. Read out the task.

 2. Check that the task is understood.

 3. Part 1: this can be answered orally. Part 2: each learner draws lines to match names to coloured shapes.

• Follow-up – you could use these questions and additional activities.

Ask for the names of other colours. Write them on the board. Ask learners to find things in the class that match the colours written on the board.

Ideas for additional activities

You could also have a set of coloured cards and a set of name cards matching them. Arrange them randomly and ask learners to pair them up – the colour name with the colour card.

Answers

• Possible answers: 1. Light colours are third and fourth; dark colours are first and second. 2. Lines connect green to first, red to second, black to third and blue to fourth.

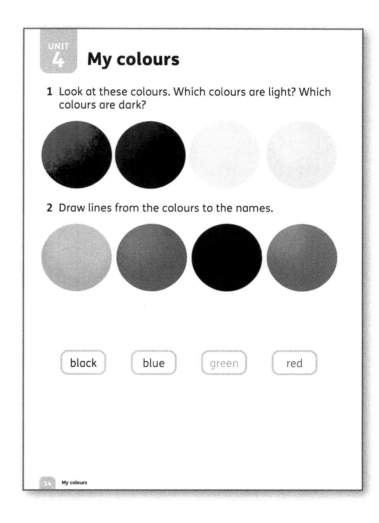

UNIT
4
My colours

1 Look at these colours. Which colours are light? Which colours are dark?

2 Draw lines from the colours to the names.

black   blue   green   red

14   My colours

Colours and shapes

Page 15

Materials needed: pencils. colouring materials, shapes and name cards that match those on the page.

Activity teaching notes:

- Warm-up: hold up the shape cards one by one and ask learners to name them. Hold up the name cards one by one and ask learners to read them. Stick cards in random order on board and ask learners to come and move the cards around to match the names to the shapes.

- Focus on the activity:

  1. Read out the task.

  2. Check that the task is understood.

  3. Learners colour shapes as the task instructs, then choose their own colours for the other shapes.

- Follow-up – you could use these questions and additional activities.

Invite learners to show what they have done. Ask them to find the colours chosen most then least by the whole class.

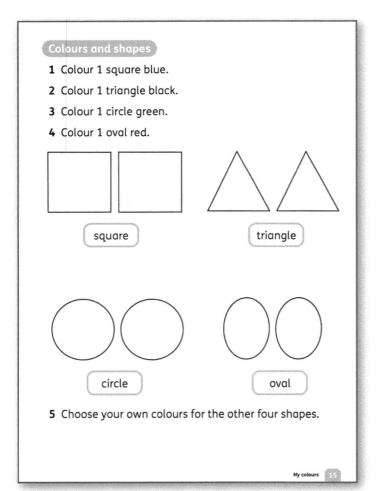

Ideas for additional activities

Repeat the warm-up task with new colour names on cards for learners to read and match with things in the room, including clothing.

Answers

- Possible answers: various colours, depending on individual learners

Clothes colours

Page 16

Materials needed:

- pencils

Activity teaching notes:

- Warm-up: remind learners of the sets they made last time. See whether they can recall the largest and the smallest groups.

- Focus on the activity:

  1. Read out the task.

  2. Check that the task is understood.

  3. Individuals count the number in each group and record their answers in the boxes correctly.

  4. Focus on the comparison of group sizes, using the comparative terms 'bigger, biggest'.

- Follow-up – you could use these questions and additional activities.

Ask learners: If a group is large what can happen?

Answers

- Possible answers: the numbers 2 to 6 should be matched to the group sizes. The biggest group is the one with 6 learners.

- Example answers:

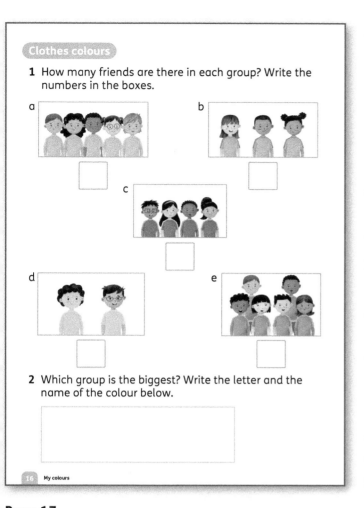

1 How many friends are there in each group? Write the numbers in the boxes.

a

b

c

d

e

2 Which group is the biggest? Write the letter and the name of the colour below.

3 Colour the clothes. Make 1 thing red, 1 thing blue, 1 thing pink and 1 thing green.

4 Which colour do you like best? Find three things of that colour.

5 Draw something in your favourite colour. Show and tell.

16 My colours

My colours 17

Page 17

Materials needed:

- pencils, colouring materials

Activity teaching notes:

- Warm-up: get learners to talk about the colours they like and don't like. Then focus on the colour of clothes.

- Focus on the activity:

  1. Read out the task.

  2. Check that the task is understood.

  3. Encourage learners to use the given colours correctly, one per child in the drawings.

  4. Extend the conversation about the colours learners like and why, if possible.

  5. Let learners move about the room and even outside if possible, to find three things to match their favourite colour. Once complete, let the class share what they have found.

  6. Individuals draw an item that is their favourite colour.

  7. The class share what they have drawn.

- Follow-up – you could use these questions and additional activities.

Ask: Is any colour more common than others? What is it? Which is the favourite colour of most people in the class?

Ideas for additional activities

Sort the class into groups on the basis of their favourite colours. Get them to count the numbers in each set. Write the colours and the numbers on the board as a record of the 'survey'.

Answers

- Possible answers: there will be various answers as this depends on individual preferences. The items found to match the favourite colours will be right or wrong.

- What drawn answers should include: each child should be coloured with one or other of the four colours named.

Learning objectives

• To name and compare items of clothing and relate them to their uses

Key words

pair, count, clothes, wear, feet, same, different, order, size, smallest, biggest, decorate

Topic introduction

• Name of topic: My clothes

• Things to talk about: have a class conversation about the choice of clothes to suit the weather and the activity.

My clothes

Page 18

Materials needed:

• pencils, colouring materials

Activity teaching notes:

• Warm-up: get learners to look at one another and find similarities and differences in the way they are dressed.

• Focus on the activity:

1. Read out the task.

2. Check that the task is understood.

3. Individuals sort out the pairs and then colour them using their own choice of colours, but making both items in the pair the same colour.

4. Counting the footwear and recording the total in the box is simple and quick.

• Follow-up – you could use these questions and additional activities.

Ask: Why are there different things we put on our feet?

Ideas for additional activities

Ask learners to compare the girls' and boys' school clothes. Ask them to identify similarities and differences.

UNIT
5 **My clothes**

1 Find the pairs.

2 Colour them. Use one colour for each pair.

3 Count the things we put on our feet. ☐

18 My clothes

Answers

- Possible answers: pairs – shoes, flip-flops, boots, socks, gloves.
- Example answers:

- What drawn answers should include: the same colour should be used for both things in a pair.

Same or different

Page 19

Materials needed:

- pencils

Activity teaching notes:

- Warm-up: get learners to look at the way they are dressed and point out differences and similarities.
- Focus on the activity:
  1. Read out the task.
  2. Check that the task is understood.
  3. Individuals mark with a tick or an X items that are the same or different. Check that they mark items correctly.

Follow-up – you could use these questions and additional activities.

- Do learners prefer everyday clothes or uniforms? Ask for explanations.

Ideas for additional activities

Learners could play sorting and matching games with clothes from the dressing-up box and/or dolls clothes.

Answers

- Possible answers: clothes of learners from one school should be marked with X and the other with ticks, boys and girls separately. Colour, style and identity of items are the bases of comparison.
- Example answers:

Same or different

1 Look at the two girls.
   Put ☒ on clothes that are different.
   Put ☑ on clothes that are the same.

2 Look at the two boys.
   Put ☒ on clothes that are different.
   Put ☑ on clothes that are the same.

My clothes 19

Page 20

Materials needed:

• pencils, colouring materials

Activity teaching notes:

• Warm-up: hold up pencils of different lengths and ask someone to arrange them in order of length. Introduce comparatives into the conversation. Repeat with books or other items.

• Focus on the activity:

  1. Read out the task.

  2. Check that the task is understood.

  3. Individuals write the numbers on items – 1 to 4 or 1 to 6. Check that they are using 1 for the smallest each time.

  4. Only the biggest in each set should be coloured.

• Follow-up – you could use these questions and additional activities.

Ask learners how they feel when they get new shoes. The experience of getting new shoes should be talked about in the context of feet getting bigger with age.

Ideas for additional activities

Let learners choose sets of items from the room that are of different sizes and ask other learners to sort them by size/length (e.g. blocks, toys, pens).

Answers

• Possible answers: each set of three or four items should be numbered from 1 for the smallest to 3 or 4 for the biggest.

3 Find the clothes which are the same type. Then, number them in order of size. Write (1) on the smallest in each set. The socks have been done for you.

4 Colour the biggest in each set.

20 My clothes

Shoes and hats

Page 21

Materials needed:

• pencils, colouring materials

Activity teaching notes:

• Warm-up: if any learners have sports shoes on or in the room get them to show them to the class and compare colours, styles and materials. Let learners discuss their preferences.

• Focus on the activity:

  1. Read out the task.

  2. Check that the task is understood.

  3. Let learners choose how they colour the shoes.

  4. Once the shoes are coloured, the hat drawing can begin with each learner choosing the type of hat to draw and to colour.

  5. Share the pictures of shoes and hats and collect learners' reactions.

• Follow-up – you could use these questions and additional activities.

Ask: What is the most common type of hat we drew? What colour was chosen by most people for the shoes?

Ideas for additional activities

Give the class a simple hat-making task, using paper, sticky tape, staples, paper clips.

Invite learners to sort the hats by shape. Hang the sets of hats from a string across the room, using paper clips or sticky tape.

Answers

• Possible answers: all answers will be different. There is no limit on the choice of colours or patterns for the shoes or hats. Let learners express themselves freely.

• What drawn answers should include: a hat of any shape and type should be coloured and decorated in some way.

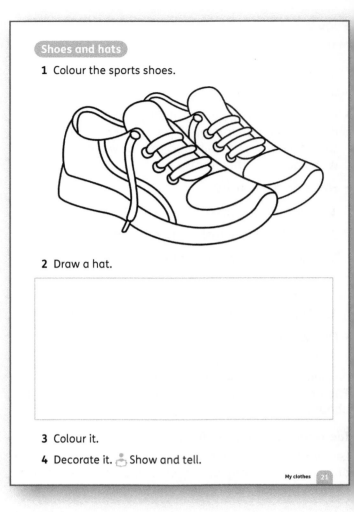

Shoes and hats

1 Colour the sports shoes.

2 Draw a hat.

3 Colour it.

4 Decorate it. Show and tell.

My clothes 21

Circles and patterns

Page 22

Materials needed:

- pencils, bricks of four colours (red, blue, yellow, green), colouring materials

Activity teaching notes:

- Warm-up: look around the room for any patterns (e.g. on the floor tiles, carpet, curtains, clothes). Let learners point them out.

- Focus on the activity:

  1. Read out the task.

  2. Check that the task is understood.

  3. Learners should colour the blocks for themselves. Monitor the continuation of the colour patterns.

  4. As learners finish the colouring let them start to make patterns using the bricks.

- Follow-up – you could use these questions and additional activities.

Ask: Which pattern was the most difficult to follow? Invite learners to try to explain why.

Ideas for additional activities

Let learners move around the room and look at the brick patterns made by one another. If they find any mistakes, get them to explain why the pattern is wrong and suggest what to change.

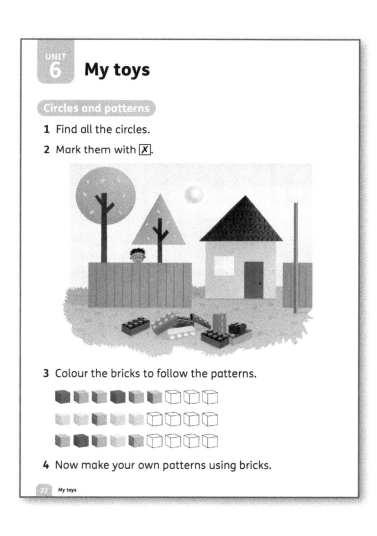

UNIT 6 **My toys**

Circles and patterns

1 Find all the circles.

2 Mark them with $\boxed{X}$.

3 Colour the bricks to follow the patterns.

4 Now make your own patterns using bricks.

22 My toys

Answers

- Possible answers: (a) red, green, blue (b) blue, yellow, yellow, blue (c) red, blue, yellow, green

- Example answers:

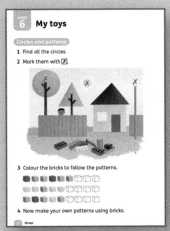

- What drawn answers should include: each brick should have been coloured correctly.

Wheels

Page 23

Materials needed:

- pencils

Activity teaching notes:

- Warm-up: ask learners to name toys that have wheels and how they can play with them.

- Focus on the activity:

  1. Read the task.

  2. Check that the task is understood.

  3. Each learner counts the wheels and writes the numbers on the lines.

  4. Ask learners to share their answers orally.

- Follow-up – use suitable questions and additional activities.

1 How many wheels? Count the wheels and write the number next to it.

Our favourite toys

Page 24

Materials needed:

- pencils, colouring materials

Activity teaching notes:

- Warm-up: let learners tell one another about toys they have at home.

- Focus on the activity:

  1. Read out the task.

  2. Check that the task is understood.

  3. Remind learners to make the drawing as large as possible and to colour it accurately.

  4. Sit class in a circle and let them all show their drawings to one another.

  5. Let them talk about their reasons for choosing that toy and the toys they dream of having.

- Follow-up – you could use these questions and additional activities.

Ask: Do you let your friends share your favourite toy? Why?

Ideas for additional activities

Invite learners to sort the drawings into sets of various kinds and talk about them (e.g. vehicles, dolls, soft toys, construction materials).

Answers

- Possible answers: each learner will decide what to draw so there are no right answers.

- What drawn answers should include: toys, chosen by learners (e.g. hard toys, soft toys, moving toys)

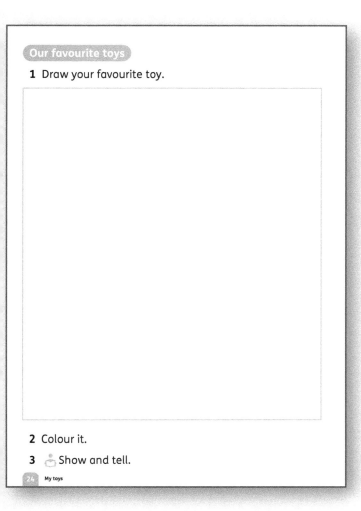

UNIT 7 My shadow

Learning objectives

- To explore and learn more about shadow formation and behaviour
- To identify the link between the sun's light and shadow formation

Key words

shadow, shape, sun, lose, play, game

Topic introduction

- Name of topic: My shadow
- Things to talk about: ask riddle-type questions to provoke learners' thinking about shadows. For example, ask: What can you lose and find on sunny days? What is sometimes beside you, sometimes behind you and sometimes in front of you?

My shadow

Page 25

Materials needed:

- none

Activity teaching notes:

- Warm-up: on a sunny day, stand learners in line along the windows, facing outwards and looking at the scene outside. Then get them to turn round and look into the room. Ask what they notice.

- Focus on the activity:

  1. Read out the task.

  2. Check that the task is understood.

  3. Let learners look at the picture and work out what the children are doing. The game may not have a name but it should be possible for learners to explain it. Encourage them to describe how it is played.

  4. If possible, go outside and let learners explore making and losing their shadows. When you are satisfied they have understood how to do that, let them play the chasing game in pairs, then in larger groups. You can devise the rules of the game any way you like.

  5. Let learners talk about how they made and lost their shadows.

- Follow-up – you could use these questions and additional activities.

Ask: Where was the best place to lose your shadow? Why?

UNIT 7 **My shadow**

1 How many shadows can you see?

2 Go outside and play the chasing shadows game.

My shadow 25

Ideas for additional activities

Stand learners in the sun on a line. Using chalk, mark each shadow's length. Return to the same line later and mark the shadows again. Encourage learners to talk about what they see and explain it.

> **Answers**
> * Possible answers: explanations will vary, with more or less understanding of the process of making and losing shadows. The main idea is that the sun's light must be falling on learners to produce a shadow. If the sun's light does not fall on them, then they 'lose' their shadow, so standing behind an object such as a wall or tree blocks the light and prevents the shadow being made.

Where is the sun?

Page 26

Materials needed:

* pencils

Activity teaching notes:

* Warm-up: recap on the game played outside and focus on shadow shapes – did they change? Could it be done on purpose? How?
* Focus on the activity:
  1. Read out the task.
  2. Check that the task is understood.
  3. Focus attention on the position of the shadows of bushes and trees before letting learners add the shadow of the building in the picture.
  4. Remind them of shapes as they draw.
  5. Let the class show their drawings to one another and talk about why they made them as they did. Try to get them to explain the relationship between the body shape and the shadow shape.
  6. Shift the focus of the conversation to the sun's position and let learners work out how that relates to the shadows.
* Follow-up – you could use these questions and additional activities.

Ask learners to think about playing the shadow game at night.

Where is the sun?

1 Look at the picture.

2 Complete the building's shadow.

26 My shadow

Ideas for additional activities

Invite the class to play shadow puppets with a lamp and a plain wall. Challenge learners to make shapes of things with their heands (e.g. a butterfly, and animal's head).

> **Answers**
> * Possible answers: learners should realise that the shadow shapes are matched to the shape of the object.
> * What drawn answers should include: the building shadow fills the outline provided.

Shadow shapes

Page 27

Materials needed:

* pencils, chalk

Activity teaching notes:

* Warm-up: recap on the task with the two shadow shapes and ask for suggestions about making other shapes.
* Focus on the activity:
  1. Read out the task.
  2. Check that the task is understood.

3. Go outside and allow each learner to experiment with making different-shaped shadows.

4. When all have managed at least four shapes, let pairs show their shapes to one another. You and other adults should draw around some with chalk. Choose a few of the more unusual for the class to see.

5. In class let each learner draw lines from the shadows matched to the children in the picture.

6. Talk about the shape changing activity, emphasising how much fun and how easy it was.

• Follow-up – you could use these questions and additional activities.

Invite learners to name other things whose shadows change.

Ideas for additional activities
Let learners choose other items from the room to try out changing the shape of their shadows, using the lamp and the plain wall.

Answers
• Possible answers: any number of possible shapes can be made, depending on the imagination of learners.

• What drawn answers should include: the four lines must link the four shadows to the four children.

Shadow shapes

You can change the shape of your shadow.

1 Draw lines from the children to their shadows.

2 Go outside and change your shadow.

3 Make four shapes.

My shadow 27

Materials needed:

• pencils, colouring materials

Activity teaching notes:

• Warm-up: let learners talk about playing the shadow game and where the best place was to lose their shadow.

• Focus on the activity:

1. Read out the task.

2. Check that the task is understood.

3. Individual learners mark their chosen places with X.

4. Let the class see one another's answers, then talk about examples where they agree or disagree.

5. Individuals add the drawing of themselves with their shadow.

• Follow-up – you could use these questions and additional activities.

Ask: Why did you have to look at the direction of the shadows in the picture?

Ideas for additional activities
Focus learners' attention on the shadows of the window frames falling on the sill and/or the floor. Let them use chalk to mark where the shadows are. Later in the day let them look again and ask what they see and how they can explain it.

Answers
• Possible answers: every X must be 'behind' a shadow in the picture.

• What drawn answers should include: the drawing of themselves with a shadow must be out in the open sunlit area and the direction of the shadow must match the others in the picture.

If you stand in the shadow of something big, you can lose your shadow!

4 Look at the picture.

5 Put ☒ where you could lose your shadow.

Learning objectives

- To be more aware of levels of sound
- To be able to use their voices in a variety of ways

Key words

voice, sing, talk, shout, whisper, message, mouth, sounds, animal

Topic introduction

- Name of topic: My voice
- Things to talk about: mime information to the class. Let them react spontaneously with comments, questions and guide the conversation round to how much we use our voices in various ways.

My voice

Page 29

Materials needed:

- pencils

Activity teaching notes:

- Warm-up: whisper to the class and gradually raise your voice in response to learners' reactions.
- Focus on the activity:
  1. Read out the task.
  2. Check that it is understood.
  3. Each learner copies the words from the box onto the lines with the pictures.
  4. Share answers from some learners, then pair them up for the whispering task.
  5. When both have whispered and spoken out loud, start the class discussion of these two ways of using their voices. Focus on the positive and negative aspects of the two. The singing of songs can be done by individuals, groups and the whole class.
- Follow-up – you could use these questions and additional activities.

Ask: When is whispering a kind thing to do? When is whispering an unkind thing to do?

UNIT
8 My voice

1 Write one of the words below each picture.

shout   sing   talk   whisper

_____   _____

_____   _____

2 Whisper to your partner. Now talk in your normal voice.

3 Take it in turns to sing each other your favourite song.

My voice 29

Ideas for additional activities

Arrange the class in a circle with yourself at the centre. Whisper a learner's name and ask learners to identify it when they think they hear it clearly. Repeat this with other names. Then ask learners to take turns.

Answers

- Possible answers: the lines should have the correct words copied from the word box.
- Example answers:

Page 30

Materials needed:

- none

Activity teaching notes:

- Warm-up: sit the class in a circle and recap on the whispering task done last time.
- Focus on the activity:

1. Read out the task.

2. Check that the task is understood. If learners have never played the game before, you need to clarify the points they raise when looking at the picture.

3. Sit in the circle and pass on the whispered message to the child next to you. Keep the message short and use familiar words.

4. When the child on your other side has received the whispered message, ask that child to say it out loud. It may or may not be the same as you gave the first child but this does not matter as it will lead to a discussion about the process and the weaknesses of whispering messages from one to another.

5. Repeat as often as it seems to engage learners. Let one of them start the message, but get them to tell you what it is before it gets passed on.

- Follow-up – you could use these questions and additional activities.

Ask: What were some of the problems in this method of passing messages?

Ideas for additional activities

Put the class into groups of four to six and play the game again. Then find out if the messages are more successfully passed on. Let learners try to explain the results.

Answers

Possible answers: the smaller number in the group means there is less chance for the message to be changed. In a smaller group, the message is more likely to be successfully sent round the circle.

4 Point to the child who is whispering.

5 Sit with a group of friends in a circle. Choose someone to think of a simple phrase. Whisper the phrase to the person to the left. That person should whisper the phrase to the person to their left until the circle is complete.

6 Did the message go all the way round the circle? Was the message the same at the end?

Loud and quiet

Page 31

Materials needed:

- pencils, colouring materials

Activity teaching notes:

- Warm-up: talk about everyday sounds. Ask learners to compare them in terms of loudness.
- Focus on the activity:

1. Read out the task.

2. Check that the task is understood.

3. Each learner should decide which pictures to colour.

4. Talk about how easy or difficult the task was.

- Follow-up – you could use these questions and additional activities.

Ask: Why are some things made to have loud sounds? Is the loud crying of a baby a good thing? Why?

Ideas for additional activities

Use instruments to make loud and quiet sounds.

Put up a screen or cloth, place a selection of musical instruments behind it and ask learners one at a time to play one of them quietly. The rest of the class try to name the instrument. Repeat this a few times as long as learners remain engaged.

Answers

- Possible answers: lightning, alarm clock, fire engine, crying baby

- Focus on the activity:
  1. Read out the task.
  2. Check that the task is understood.
  3. Learners should share their ideas of the sounds made by the animals and objects shown, then in pairs challenge one another to identify the sounds made at random.
  4. Open up this activity to the whole class and let individual learners make a sound for the class to name. Then let learners choose animals or other sound makers not shown in the pictures and ask the class to name them.
  5. Each learner draws a picture of a sound maker in the space provided and the class share their drawings.

- Follow-up – you could use these questions and additional activities.

Ask: Why do animals make sounds? What is the main difference between their sounds and ours?

Ideas for additional activities

Play recordings of animal sounds and ask learners to name them. Ask learners to mimic the animal sounds. Let individual learners, one at a time, choose an animal to mimic. Each learner tells you – but not the other learners – what the animal is. The class has to identify it.

Answers

- Possible answers: the sounds made will vary enormously; some will be more accurate than others.
- What drawn answers should include: answers will depend on what learners choose to draw. Check that all show sound makers.

Sounds and noises

Page 32

Materials needed:

- pencils, colouring materials

Activity teaching notes:

- Warm-up: mimic the sound of a familiar animal and ask learners to name it. Repeat with several different animals, but do not use any included in the task.

1 Use your voice to make the sounds for the pictures.
Point to the picture as you make the sound.

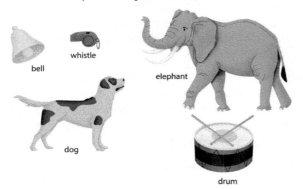

bell

whistle

elephant

dog

drum

2 Make more animal noises. Ask others to name them.

3 Draw another thing that makes a noise.
 Show and tell.

My feelings

Learning objectives

• To identify and describe various feelings

Key words

feelings, face, sad, happy, angry, excited, tired, afraid, name, show

Topic introduction

• Name of topic: My feelings

• Things to talk about: the unit is about subjective experiences learners all have but do not always have the language or self-awareness to express. This unit gives them both the words and the opportunity to reflect on the range of feelings they have. A conversation can be started simply by asking the class how they feel today and let the answers come as they will. The tasks focus attention on how we communicate feelings through our faces.

My feelings

Page 33

Materials needed:

• pencils

Activity teaching notes:

• Warm-up: ask what else we do to express how we feel apart from what our faces reveal. Accept all ideas and see who agrees or disagrees with them.

• Focus on the activity:

1. Read out the task.

2. Check that the task is understood.

3. Let learners look at the picture in pairs and talk about it, looking in particular at how people are feeling and how they are showing it.

4. Let the class hear the ideas from the pairs and allow differences of opinion. Ask learners to give evidence to support their ideas; i.e. refer to the behaviour of children in the picture.

5. Ask individuals to show feelings using more than just their faces. Ask others to identify the feelings.

• Follow-up – you could use these questions and additional activities.

Ask: Which is easier to show with your behaviour – being sad or being excited? Why?

UNIT **9** My feelings

Feelings

sad   angry   excited   tired   afraid

1 What do you think the children are feeling?

2 In pairs, talk about the feelings. Do you agree with your partner?

My feelings 33

Ideas for additional activities

Encourage learners to talk about how they deal with negative feelings (e.g. sadness, fear or anger).

Answers
- Possible answers: the picture includes children who are expressing happiness and excitement by clapping, cheering, jumping up and down and holding up their hands. Others are sitting with drooping shoulders and sad face or standing 'outside' the group fun, looking afraid. These are the behaviours you hope learners will cite as evidence of feelings.

Page 34

Materials needed:

- pencils

Activity teaching notes:

- Warm-up: ask about feelings when playing with toys or when tired, sad or alone.

- Focus on the activity:

  1. Read out the task.

  2. Check that the task is understood.

  3. Let pairs look at the picture and decide what the children are feeling.

  4. Each pair should copy the words that match their answers.

  5. Let pairs report to the class what they have written.

- Follow-up – you could use these questions and additional activities.

Encourage the learners to question one another about how they identified the feelings in the picture.

Ideas for additional activities

Ask learners to mime feelings for the rest of the class to identify.

3 What do you think the children are feeling?

Feelings

sad   angry   happy   tired   afraid

4 In pairs, write the names of the feelings.

_____

_____

34   My feelings

Page 35

Materials needed:

• pencils, colouring materials

Activity teaching notes:

• Warm-up: ask for examples of when learners were upset by something.

• Focus on the activity:

1. Read out the task.

2. Check that the task is understood.

3. As a class, look at the pictures and talk about the three situations one by one, moving on from one to another when everyone has had the chance to say what they think.

4. Each time ask for the 'clues' – the evidence learners are using to identify the feelings.

5. Make the conversation personal by asking what makes individuals sad, then getting them to draw their sad, angry or afraid face.

6. Let learners hold up their drawings and ask the class to identify the feelings shown in them.

• Follow-up – you could use these questions and additional activities.

Ask: What cheers you up when you are feeling sad? Have you felt angry or lonely at school? What did you do about those feelings?

Answers

• Possible answers: individuals will interpret the three situations in their own way, but if they are totally 'misreading' them, use the answers of other learners to challenge those ideas.

• What drawn answers should include: a variety of faces showing one of the three emotions – sadness, anger, fear

---

5 What do you think the children are feeling? How can you tell?

6 What makes you sad, angry or afraid? Draw a feeling. Show and tell.

My feelings 35

Feeling happy

Page 36

Materials needed:

- pencils, colouring materials

Activity teaching notes:

- Warm-up: invite learners to tell the class about happy things that have happened to them and why they made them feel happy.

- Focus on the activity:

  1. Read out the task.

  2. Check that the task is understood.

  3. Individuals choose what to include in their picture, but they must include themselves somewhere.

  4. Sit in a circle and show one another the pictures. Ask one or two learners to talk about their pictures, then pair them and let them talk to one another about what they have drawn.

- Follow-up – you could use these questions and additional activities.

Ask: What can others do to make you happy? What can you do to make someone else happy?

Ideas for additional activities

Encourage learners to act out narratives where one person does something that makes another happy. Use learners' own ideas for these short 'plays'.

Answers

- Possible answers: the words should be traced in pencil or colouring material.

- What drawn answers should include: each picture will be unique, but should contain obvious signs of happiness – shown in faces, behaviour.

Learning objectives

- To understand some of the ways they can protect their health
- To know that diet and exercise are important for good health

Key words

health, teeth, clean, wash, dry, run, swim, jump, climb, ride, meal, foods, eat

Topic introduction

- Name of topic: My health
- Things to talk about: let learners share their experiences of being unwell.

My health

Page 37

Materials needed:

- pencils

Activity teaching notes:

- Warm-up: ask learners to tap on their teeth and then to open and close their jaws rapidly to bang their teeth together.
- Focus on the activity:
  1. Read out the task.
  2. Check that the task is understood.
  3. Each learner draws teeth in the 'empty' mouth.
  4. The placing of the ticks may vary as different learners may use different ways of cleaning their teeth.
  5. Let learners explain to the class how they use the cleaning items.
  6. Counting can be done by touching the teeth with fingertips and/or by looking into a mirror.
  7. The number will vary across the class and some learners may need help with writing it down as it is relatively large.
- Follow-up – you could use these questions and additional activities.

Ask: Why do some of you have gaps in your teeth?

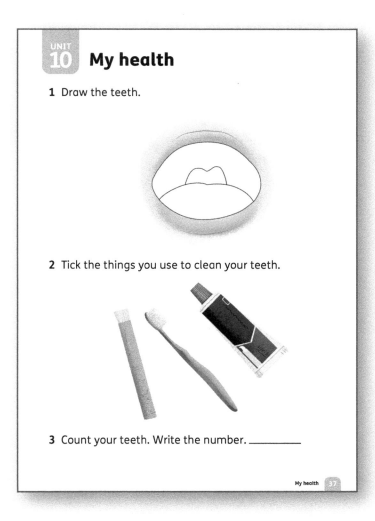

UNIT 10 **My health**

1 Draw the teeth.

2 Tick the things you use to clean your teeth.

3 Count your teeth. Write the number. _____

My health 37

Ideas for additional activities

Collect the tooth numbers from the class and write them on the board. Various processes can be carried out – sorting into sets, arranging in order, turning into a block chart showing frequency. Ask learners to compare the numbers and talk about the differences.

Answers

- Possible answers: cleaning items may vary across the class, so ticks will vary. The number of teeth will also vary, up to a maximum of 20.
- What drawn answers should include: the teeth may not be accurately drawn in sizes or numbers but that is not important.

Washing

Page 38

Materials needed:

- toys, water, bowls, towels, soap, washcloths

Activity teaching notes:

- Warm-up: what do we do each day, usually in the morning before we come to school? Various answers, including washing, will be given.
- Focus on the activity:
  1. Read out the task.
  2. Check that the task is understood.
  3. As a class, look at the picture and talk about what it shows.
  4. Put the class into pairs or small groups and give them the things they need to demonstrate washing and drying. Encourage them to talk as they do the task.
  5. Once the toys are put to one side, ask learners to wash their hands and dry them.
- Follow-up – you could use these questions and additional activities.

Ask: When is it important to wash our hands? (before eating and after going to the toilet)

Ideas for additional activities

Have a class discussion about the reasons to keep clean and the connections with being unwell.

Answers

- Possible answers: ticks for before eating, after playing outdoors, after going to the toilet
- Example answers:

Washing

1 Choose a toy. Wash your toy. Dry it.

2 Now wash your hands. Dry them.

3 Tick the boxes. When must you wash your hands?

Before		/ After		eating.
Before		/ After		playing outdoors.
Before		/ After		going to the toilet.

38 My health

Exercise

Page 39

Materials needed:

- pencils, colouring materials

Activity teaching notes:

- Warm-up: which do you like best – just sitting all day long or moving about playing?
- Focus on the activity:

  1. Read out the task.

  2. Check that the task is understood.

  3. Individuals should look at the pictures on their own and tick the things they do. Most should tick all or most of them. Have a brief feedback conversation before taking the class outside.

  4. Encourage learners to do as many of the activities as possible (probably not swimming).

  5. Back in class individuals draw pictures that will be very personal to them.

  6. When they finish drawing, sit the class in a circle and let everyone show their pictures and talk about them.

- Follow-up – you could use these questions and additional activities.

Ask: Why is it important to make our bodies active in these ways?

Ideas for additional activities

Outside, involve learners in some sort of class game of chasing or catching one another.

Answers

- Possible answers: the ticks will vary across the class. Many may not yet swim and some may not like to climb.

- What drawn answers should include: pictures will vary, but should all include the individual doing the various activities shown.

Exercise

1 Look at the ways of taking exercise. Tick all the things you do.

2 Draw your favourite way of taking exercise. Show and tell.

My health 39

Food

Page 40

Materials needed:

• pencils, colouring materials

Activity teaching notes:

• Warm-up: what are your favourite foods? Explain why.

• Focus on the activity:

  1. Read out the task.

  2. Check that the task is understood.

  3. Each meal will be personal to the individual. What learners choose to draw is for them to decide.

  4. Individuals should circle the foods they eat and when all are done, get the class to talk about those foods – how often they eat them, what do they like/dislike about them, etc.

  5. Ask some learners to show their drawings.

• Follow-up – you could use this question and suitable additional activities.

Ask: What foods would you like to try for the first time? Explain why.

Answers

• Possible answers: the circling of foods will be personal.

• What drawn answers should include: the meals should be as complete as possible, with at least three foods.

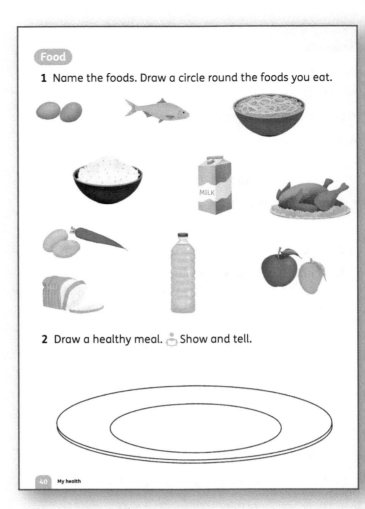

Food

1 Name the foods. Draw a circle round the foods you eat.

2 Draw a healthy meal. Show and tell.

40 My health

Learning objectives

- To recognise and name the different ways pets move
- To identify and name various common pets
- To understand that foods and homes must be matched to pets

Key words

pets, legs, count, cat, dog, fish, tortoise, parrot, rabbit, canary, foods, order, size, move, swim, fly, walk, run, hop, home

Topic introduction

- Name of topic: My pets
- Things to talk about: explore the feelings learners have towards sharing their homes with animals of various kinds.

My pets

Page 41

Materials needed:

- pencils

Activity teaching notes:

- Warm-up: ask learners to name as many kinds of pet animal as possible. Write their answers on the board.

- Focus on the activity:

  1. Read out the task.

  2. Check that the task is understood.

  3. Learners should draw lines from words to drawings.

  4. The number of legs for each animal should be written beside its name.

  5. Have a class discussion about the pets in the pictures and let learners share their experiences.

- Follow-up – you could use these questions and additional activities.

Ask: Which pets need very little attention from you or your family? Explain why.

Ideas for additional activities

Collect the leg numbers on the board and carry out various processes, such as ordering them, putting them into sets and drawing a block chart.

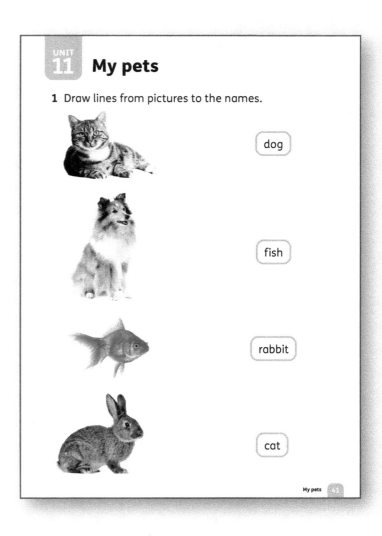

UNIT 11 **My pets**

1 Draw lines from pictures to the names.

dog

fish

rabbit

cat

My pets 41

Answers

- Possible answers: the lines should connect the names to the drawings correctly. The leg numbers are: cat, dog, rabbit – all four; fish – zero.

- Example answers:

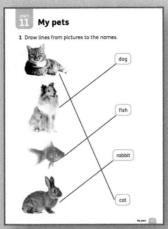

- What drawn answers should include: each name should have one line connecting it to a drawing.

Food for pets

Page 42

Materials needed:

- pencils, colouring materials

Activity teaching notes:

- Warm-up: what do we have to do for all our pets?

- Focus on the activity:

  1. Read out the task.

  2. Check that the task is understood.

  3. Individuals draw a pet they have or they want and write its name on the drawing.

  4. The foods then have to be selected from the list to match the pet in the drawing and marked by ticks.

  5. Once all are ready, have a class sharing time when learners talk about how they feed their pets – how often, when in the day, etc.

- Follow-up – you could use these questions and additional activities.

Ask: What happens when you give the wrong food to your pet?

Ideas for additional activities

Ask those with pets to explain what happens if the family go away on holiday.

Answers

- Possible answers: these will vary depending on the choices of the learners. Check that the foods are matched to the pets.

- What drawn answers should include: these will vary depending on the choices of the learners.

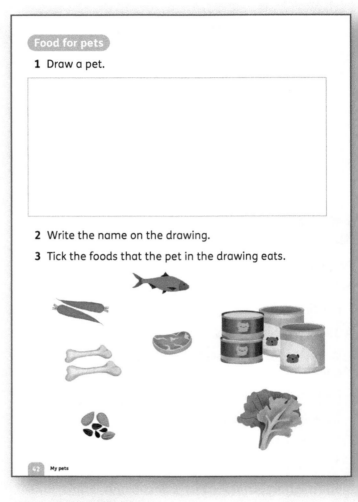

Pets in motion

Page 43

Materials needed:

- pencils

Activity teaching notes:

- Warm-up: have a conversation about how we humans can move about. Collect answers on the board.

- Focus on the activity:

  1. Read out the task.

  2. Check that the task is understood.

  3. Individuals should draw the lines for themselves, connecting the drawings to the movements.

4. As a class, discuss the movements of animals.

5. Outside, let learners choose to mimic the movements of animals as well as move themselves in various ways.

6. Flying and swimming require imagination as well as skill so commend those who produce good simulations.

• Follow-up – you could use these questions and additional activities.

Ask: Why can fish swim better than we can? Why can birds fly and we cannot fly?

Ideas for additional activities

Let individuals move as a particular animal and ask the class to identify them.

Answers

• Possible answers: swim – fish; fly – parrot: walk – parrot, tortoise, dog, mouse, rabbit; run – dog, mouse, rabbit; hop – rabbit

Pets in motion

1 Draw lines from pets to the words about movement.

hop

swim

run

walk

fly

2 Go outside. Move in different ways – run, walk and hop.

3 Pretend to fly and swim.

Homes for pets

Page 44

Materials needed:

• pencils, colouring materials

Activity teaching notes:

• Warm-up: ask learners to talk about pets they have and where they are kept inside or outside the house.

• Focus on the activity:

1. Read through the task.

2. Check that the task is understood.

3. Individuals connect the pets to their homes with lines.

4. Remind learners to draw the pet home as large as they can in the space on the page.

5. Let learners show their drawings and answer questions from the class.

• Follow-up – you could use these questions and additional activities?

Ask: Why do some homes have bars? Can you think of other pet animals kept in cages?

Ideas for additional activities

Invite learners to name some pets that are free to move around inside and outside the house.

Answers

• Possible answers: fish/aquarium, dog/basket, birds/cage, hamster/box cage, rabbit/ hutch

• What drawn answers should include: the homes will all be different and will be chosen by learners.

1 Draw lines from the pets to their homes.

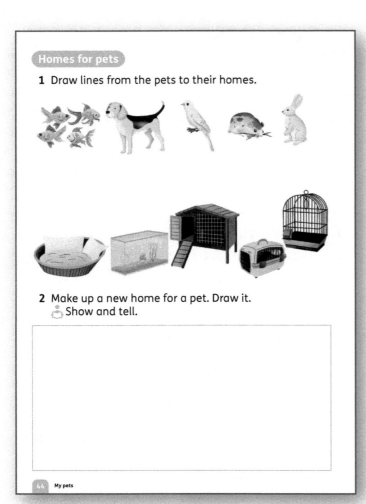

2 Make up a new home for a pet. Draw it.
Show and tell.

Learning objectives

- To identify, name and match rooms and their contents, identifying some characteristics

Key words

live, home, room, kitchen, bathroom, bedroom, living room, circle, round, soft, hard

Topic introduction

- Name of topic: Where I live
- Things to talk about: let learners tell one another about their homes and answer questions.

This is where I live

Page 2

Materials needed:

- pencils, colouring materials

Activity teaching notes:

- Warm-up: ask learners to name differences between rooms at home.
- Focus on the activity:

  1. Read out the task.
  2. Check that the task is understood.
  3. Remind learners to fill the space on the page.
  4. Individuals draw their home and colour it.
  5. In pairs, the pictures are shared and talked about.

- Follow-up – you could use these questions and additional activities.

Let the class show their drawings to one another. Ask questions involving comparisons (e.g. Which has the most windows)?

Ideas for additional activities

Invite learners to sort the drawings into sets (e.g. apartments, detached houses, terraced houses). They can then count them and find the largest set.

Answers

- What drawn answers should include: the drawing of each home should be as detailed as possible. The choice of perspective will be the choice of each learner. Some may choose to show the external and others the internal view.

UNIT 1 This is where I live

1 Draw your home.

2 Colour it.

3 Talk about your drawing with a partner.

2 This is where I live

Hard things and soft things

Page 3

Materials needed:

• pencils

Activity teaching notes:

• Warm-up: ask learners to identify soft and hard objects in the classroom.

• Focus on the activity:

  1. Read out the task.

  2. Check that the task is understood.

  3. Learners carry out the task independently.

• Follow-up – you could use these questions and additional activities.

Ask why soft things are found more in some rooms and not others.

Ideas for additional activities

Gather a selection of items from the room, randomly arranged on a table and ask learners to sort them into hard and soft sets. Ask how they decide which set to put them in. Use the words 'sense of touch'. Explore learners' ideas of where the sense of touch is located in the body – is it only in the fingers? Ask them to close their eyes and test other areas of skin to find out whether they can detect soft and hard.

Answers

• Possible answers: X should be on floors, cupboards, table, cooker, bath, toilet, drawers, lamp, shelf, wall, taps, windows, fan. Circles should be on towels, curtains, cushions, pillows, bed, rug, sofa and chair, pouffe, sheets, duvet, carpet

• Example answers:

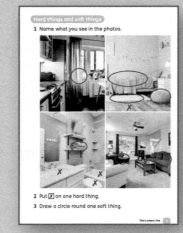

Hard things and soft things

1 Name what you see in the photos.

2 Put ☒ on one hard thing.

3 Draw a circle round one soft thing.

This is where I live 3

Rooms

Page 4

Materials needed:

• pencils, colouring materials

Activity teaching notes:

• Warm-up: ask learners to talk about different rooms at home, including what each room has in it and why.

• Focus on the activity:

  1. Read out the task.

  2. Check that the task is understood.

  3. Remind learners to use the full space for the four drawings.

  4. Let learners look at one another's drawings and find one with different objects. Let them pair up and talk about their drawings.

• Follow-up – you could use these questions and additional activities.

Hold up drawings, photos or toy versions of household items and ask learners to say which room each would be found in. For example, show a cooking pot, toilet roll and a bottle of shampoo.

1 Draw one thing you have in each room at home.

kitchen	bedroom
bathroom	living room

2 Find someone who has drawn a different thing in one of the rooms. Talk about your drawings.

This is where I live

Ideas for additional activities

Invite learners to use toy furniture, etc., to make models of different rooms. Each group could make a model of a different room.

Answers
- What drawn answers should include: the items will be very varied, depending on the learners' choices. Check that the objects are in the correct rooms.

In and out, up and down

Page 5

Materials needed:

- pencils, colouring materials

Activity teaching notes:

- Warm-up: ask learners to talk about their homes in general, without focusing on their feelings.

- Focus on the activity:

  1. Read out the task.

  2. Check that the task is understood.

---

3. Individuals should tick the items they have at home.

4. X should be added to the things that help people to go up from the ground.

5. The drawing should fill the space and each learner is free to choose what it shows.

6. Let the class see one another's drawings.

- Follow-up – you could use these questions and additional activities.

Encourage the learners to ask one another questions about the drawings, especially about why the chosen thing is the favourite.

Ideas for additional activities
Talk about the gate and the patio doors: what do they allow us to do? Ask for other examples from home that have the same function.

Answers
- Possible answers: ticks will vary from learner to learner. X should be on the stairs and the lift.
- What drawn answers should include: these will be very varied, depending on learners' choices.

In and out, up and down

1 Tick the things you have at home.

2 Put ☒ on the things that help us go up from the ground.

3 Draw your favourite thing about where you live.
Show and tell.

This is where I live

Learning objectives

- To identify and name various activities
- To sort items on the basis of colour

Key words

school, girls, boys, uniform, blue, green, brown, play, game, like, dislike, best, most

Topic introduction

- Name of topic: My school
- Things to talk about: encourage learners to talk freely about their school, expressing opinions as well as describing the place and the activities.

This is my school

Page 6

Materials needed:

- pencils, colouring materials

Activity teaching notes:

- Warm-up: learners compare the picture with their classroom, pointing out differences and similarities.
- Focus on the activity:
  1. Read out the task.
  2. Check that the task is understood.
  3. Remind learners to use all the space in the picture. Individuals are free to add as many other people to the picture as they want.
  4. Let the class share the finished drawings.
- Follow-up – you could use these questions and additional activities.

Ask learners to compare the drawings in various ways. For example: which ones have the most people? Which ones have no adults? Which one has the most people sitting down/ standing up?

Ideas for additional activities

Talk about other places in school where the number of people is more or less than shown in their classroom drawings (e.g. playground, assembly hall, office, toilets).

Answers

- What drawn answers should include: each learner chooses the number and identity of people to add to the drawing, so drawings will be very varied.

UNIT 2 This is my school

1 Draw people at school.

6 This is my school

How many?

Page 7

Materials needed:

- pencils, colouring materials

Activity teaching notes:

- Warm-up: look at the picture and ask learners to compare it with their own classroom – looking at rows, table groups, numbers, boys and/or girls.

- Focus on the activity:

  1. Read out the task.
  2. Check that the task is understood.
  3. Remind learners that they can choose how to complete the faces and show girls or boys.

- Follow-up – you could use these questions and additional activities.

Collate on the board the number of boys and girls in the pictures. Ask learners to arrange them in order from the least to the most. Compare the totals for girls and boys. Ask learners to talk about why they chose to draw what they did.

Ideas for additional activities

Using model figures, dolls or soft toys, ask learners to arrange them in different ways; grouping them in as many different ways as they can think of (e.g. all together, separated from one another totally, in circular groups of various sizes).

How many?

1 How many children in each row?

2 Write the numbers. Count from the front row.

_____ _____ _____

3 Complete the drawings.

How many girls? _____

How many boys? _____

This is my school 7

School activities

Page 8

Materials needed:

- pencils

Activity teaching notes:

- Warm-up: let learners talk about what they like and dislike about activities in school

- Focus on the activity:

  1. Read out the task.
  2. Check that the task is understood.
  3. Let the pairs look at the picture and talk about what it shows.
  4. Individuals choose their favourite activity and circles it.

- Follow-up – you could use these questions and additional activities.

Let learners tell one another why they have chosen the particular activity. What makes it their favourite?

Ideas for additional activities

Invite learners to suggest other activities not shown in the picture. Collate and total the numbers for each of the activities circled by learners and ask learners to arrange them in order of popularity. For example, which one is liked most? Which one is liked least?

1 Talk to a partner about what you see in the picture.

2 Draw a circle round the activity you like most.

8 This is my school

Answers

• Example answers: individuals will add what they want, so the drawings will be very varied.

• What drawn answers should include: individuals will add what they want, so the drawings will be very varied.

3 Draw children playing with three different things.

4 Colour the drawing. Show and tell.

This is my school 9

Page 9

Materials needed:

• pencils, colouring materials

Activity teaching notes:

• Warm-up: encourage learners to talk about outdoor play, at school, at home and in the park.

• Focus on the activity:

1. Read out the task.

2. Check that the task is understood.

3. Each learner is free to choose the three activities.

4. Let the class show their drawings to one another.

• Follow-up – you could use these questions and additional activities.

Ask learners to explain why they chose the three activities. Encourage them to talk about their feelings when doing the things shown in the picture.

Ideas for additional activities

Let learners suggest other outdoor activities not shown in the picture. Go outside and use whatever equipment is available.

UNIT 3

Books and pictures

Learning objectives

- To match numbers and objects
- To name and draw fruits and animals
- To make a simple book with pictures

Key words

book, make, fruit, animal, draw, alphabet, page, read, number, banana, stone, leaves, bean, choose

Topic introduction

- Name of topic: Books and pictures
- Things to talk about: let learners talk about books they have at home and at school, expressing opinions and feelings about them as well as naming and describing them.

Books and pictures

Page 10

Materials needed:

- pencils, paper, stapler, colouring materials

Activity teaching notes:

- Warm-up: let each learner take a book and look at how it is constructed – including groups of pages, stapled or stitched together, a cover. Encourage them to talk about what they can see.

- Focus on the activity:

  1. Read out the task.

  2. Check that the task is understood.

  3. Help learners to fold the sheets of paper one at a time and to fit them together.

  4. Staple the books and return them for learners to complete.

  5. Individuals should be left to choose the title and the contents of their books. Give time for drawings to be added to at least two pages then stop the task and let learners show their work to one another.

- Follow-up – you could use these questions and additional activities.

Let learners talk about their books.

UNIT 3 Books and pictures

1 Following the steps shown here, make a book.

a) Fold some pieces of paper. **b)** Arrange them like this.

c) Ask an adult to staple the pages together. **d)** Give the book a title.

e) Draw pictures inside.

2 Show and tell.

10 Books and pictures

Ideas for additional activities

If learners want to add text to the pages, help them by writing the words they need on the board or in faint dots in their books. Allow time for other pages to be completed.

> **Answers**
> - What drawn answers should include: this will vary from learner to learner. Drawings and words should relate in some way. The books may try to tell a story from page to page, or be a collection of factual images plus words, such as the names of the objects in the drawings.

Reading books

Page 11

Materials needed:

- none

Activity teaching notes:

- Warm-up: have a class discussion about what learners like about books in general – the pictures, the information, the stories, etc.

- Focus on the activity:

  1. Read out the task.

  2. Check that the task is understood.

  3. Allow learners to find a partner, or put them into pairs.

  4. Keep their conversations on track – what books they like and where they like to read.

- Follow-up – you could use these questions and additional activities.

Bring the class together and collate on the board the books they like. Total them. Ask learners to identify the most popular books and the least popular books. Do the same with the places where learners like to read.

Ideas for additional activities

Let the class choose a book from the classroom for you to read to them. The book should be factual or a story about some aspect of the natural world (e.g. growing plants, space travel or fishing).

> **Answers**
> - Possible answers: these will vary across the pairs. The books learners choose may be stories or factual. It does not matter either way. The places for reading books can include cosy, private places at home, in the garden, in bed, on the bus coming to school, etc.

Reading books

1 Work with a partner. What kind of books does your partner like?

2 Where do you like to read?

Books and pictures 11

Getting information

Page 12

Materials needed:

- pencils, colouring materials

Activity teaching notes:

- Warm-up: set out a selection of books in front of the learners, including story books, information books and a dictionary, randomly arranged. Ask learners to sort them into three sets and to identify the three types of book.

- Focus on the activity:

  1. Read out the task.

  2. Check that the task is understood.

  3. Ask learners to identify the animals shown. Remind them to fill the space for their drawing of an animal with a name starting with 'a', which they can choose for themselves.

- Follow-up – you could use these questions and additional activities.

Ask learners to show their drawings to one another and talk about them. Encourage learners ask questions.

Ideas for additional activities

Choose a selection of other initial letters and ask learners to name animals with names starting with those letters. Show pictures of single animals and ask learners to give the initial letters of their names.

Answers

- Possible answers: the names depend on the picture shown on the page.

- What drawn answers should include: the drawings will vary. Check that the names all start with 'a'.

Getting information

1 A dictionary is a type of book which gives us information.

2 Name the animals you can see.

3 Draw an animal beginning with the letter **a**.
   Show and tell.

An alphabet book

Page 13

Materials needed:

- pencils, colouring materials

Activity teaching notes:

- Warm-up: hold up a picture dictionary showing a selection of pages with words starting with various letters. Ask learners to identify the initial letters.

- Focus on the activity:

  1. Read out the task.

  2. Check that the task is understood.

  3. Each learner chooses to draw fruits with initials 'a' or 'b'. Remind learners to make their drawings as large as possible.

- Follow-up – you could use these questions and additional activities.

Ask learners to share their drawings and talk about them.

Ideas for additional activities

Choose a selection of other initial letters and ask learners to name fruits that have names starting with those letters. Show pictures of single fruits and ask learners to give the initial letters of their names.

Answers

- What drawn answers should include: all fruits should have 'a' or 'b' as initial letters.

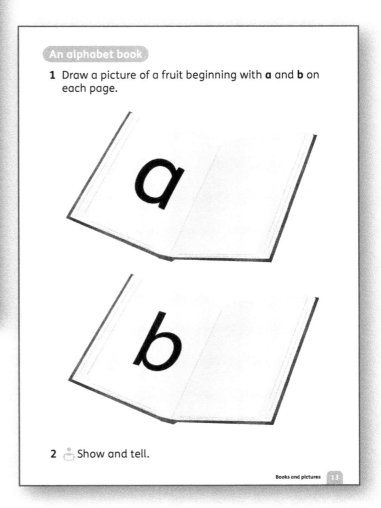

An alphabet book

1 Draw a picture of a fruit beginning with **a** and **b** on each page.

2 Show and tell.

Clocks

Learning objectives

- To know the order and position of the numerals on a clock face
- To pair the two forms of clock times and to count minutes
- To match activities to the times of the day

Key words

clock, number, time, pair, hands, minutes, underline

Topic introduction

- Name of topic: Clocks
- Things to talk about: have a general conversation about time, clocks, times of the day.

Clocks

Page 14

Materials needed:

- pencils

Activity teaching notes:

- Warm-up: explore what learners understand about clocks – the hands, their movements, the numbers and what they mean.

- Focus on the activity:

  1. Read out the task.

  2. Check that the task is understood.

  3. Give learners time to add the numerals to the clock. Check that the order is correct.

  4. All learners need to be able to see a real clock to do the second part of the task. Check the answers one by one as you move around.

  5. Let learners choose partners or put them into pairs. The talk should be focused on favourite times of the day.

- Follow-up – you could use these questions and additional activities.

Let learners tell one another about their favourite times and explain why. Use a toy clock to let learners show their chosen times on the clock face.

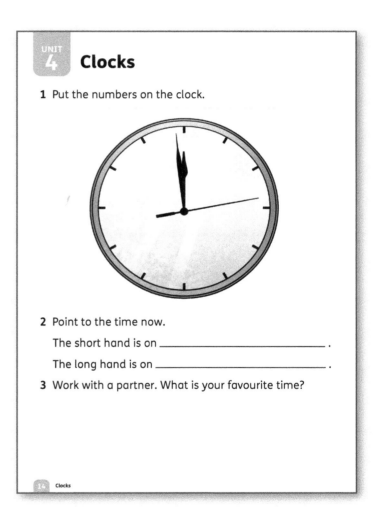

UNIT 4 Clocks

1 Put the numbers on the clock.

2 Point to the time now.

The short hand is on _____ .

The long hand is on _____ .

3 Work with a partner. What is your favourite time?

14 Clocks

Ideas for additional activities

Set the hands on the toy clock. Ask learners to 'read' the time and say what they would be doing at that time of day.

> **Answers**
> • Possible answers: the numerals should all be in the correct places next to the lines marked on the clock face.

What time?

Page 15

Materials needed:

• pencils

Activity teaching notes:

• Warm-up: have a class discussion about the changing times of a day and what learners are generally doing as a day goes by.

• Focus on the activity:

1. Read out the task.

2. Check that the task is understood.

3. Ask learners to say what each picture shows to ensure that they are being interpreted correctly.

4. Remind learners to look at the classroom clock as they fill in the four times under the pictures.

• Follow-up – you could use these questions and additional activities.

Collate the times written by learners for each of the four activities on the board. Ask learners to find patterns in the answers – are any very different? What is the most common time for each activity?

Ideas for additional activities

Randomly arrange cards on the table, each card with a time (in hours only) written on it. Ask learners to arrange them in order from the earliest to the latest.

> **Answers**
> • Possible answers: accept any time that seems reasonable for each scenario shown. The use of 'a.m.' and 'p.m.' cannot be expected but 24-hour clock times may be written by some learners.

What time?

1 What time do you do these things?

2 Put the times in the boxes.

Clocks 15

Page 16

Materials needed:

• pencils

Activity teaching notes:

• Warm-up: using the toy clock, set the hands in different positions to explore how much learners understand the role of the minute hand. Ask learners to read the times you set.

• Focus on the activity:

1. Read out the task.

2. Check that the task is understood.

3. Allow learners time to decide the time they want to show. Encourage them to use both hands if possible.

4. Put learners into pairs or allow them to choose partners. Let them talk about their clocks and identify the times shown.

• Follow-up – you could use these questions and additional activities.

The whole class displays their clocks and learners are chosen by you to read the times shown.

Ideas for additional activities

Use the toy clock to set a range of times including half hours for learners to read.

3 Draw the hands on the clock. You choose the time.

4 Work with a partner.
Show and tell.

5 Ask and answer. What time is it?

16 Clocks

Learning objectives

- To identify, name and draw common fruits and vegetables and other foods
- To sort and count sets of kitchen items
- To identify dangers in the kitchen

Key words

food, home, banana, orange, lemon, fruit, cut, share, count, plates, yellow, bowl, blue, tumbler, knives, red, green, danger, plant

Topic introduction

- Name of topic: Food
- Things to talk about: encourage learners to talk about what happens at home in the kitchen, with the focus on food preparation.

Time for food

Page 17

Materials needed:

- pencils

Activity teaching notes:

- Warm-up: let learners talk about meals they enjoy and why.
- Focus on the activity:
  1. Read out the task.
  2. Check that the task is understood.
  3. Oral answers to the first step of the task will be shared by all.
  4. The X marks should be drawn by each learner independently.
- Follow-up – you could use these questions and additional activities.

Ask learners to say where other foods come from (e.g. milk, cheese, yogurt, hens, fish).

Ideas for additional activities

Show pictures or photos of various foods one by one and ask learners to put them in the 'plants' set or the 'not plants' set.

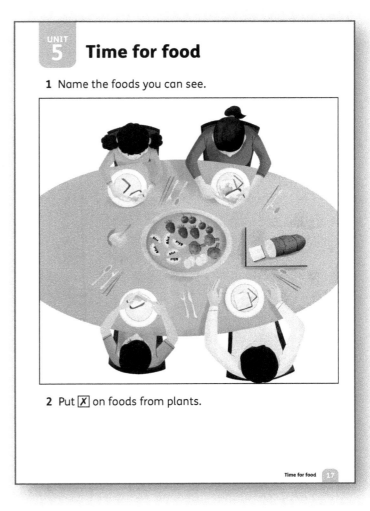

UNIT 5 Time for food

1 Name the foods you can see.

2 Put X on foods from plants.

Time for food 17

Answers

- Possible answers: all fruits and vegetables, plus bread and rice should be marked with an X.
- Example answers:

Answers

- Example answers:

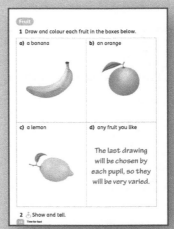

- What drawn answers should include: the drawings should be coloured correctly and be roughly the right shape. The last drawing will be chosen by each learner, so these drawings will be very varied.

Fruit

Page 18

Materials needed:

- pencils, colouring materials

Activity teaching notes:

- Warm-up: let learners talk about fruits they have eaten and their opinions of them.
- Focus on the activity:
  1. Read out the task.
  2. Check that the task is understood.
  3. Give learners time to choose and draw a fruit after drawing and colouring the three named fruits.
- Follow-up – you could use these questions and additional activities.

The class show their drawings and ask one another why they chose the fourth fruit and whether it is their favourite.

Ideas for additional activities

Ask for names of fruits that are the same colour as bananas, oranges and some of the fruits learners chose to draw. Collate answers on the board and total each set. Ask: Which colour is most common? What other colours could be added to the list? What examples can the class give for these other colours?

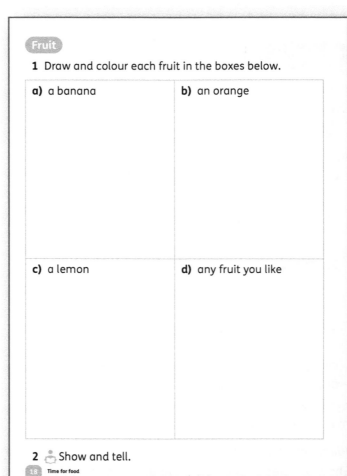

Sets and colours

Page 19

Materials needed:

• pencils, colouring materials

Activity teaching notes:

• Warm-up: talk about sorting things at home – toys, clothes, dishes, etc.

• Focus on the activity:
  1. Read out the task.
  2. Check that the task is understood.
  3. The six figures resulting from the counting should be written on the correct lines.
  4. The space on the table is small so the drawings of three foods will need to be small.

• Follow-up – you could use these questions and additional activities.

Ask: Which set has the most items? Which set has the least items? Invite learners to put the sets in order, from the smallest to the largest. Collate the drawn fruits on the board and total each one. Ask learners to compare the totals and find the most and least frequent fruits.

Ideas for additional activities

Encourage learners to colour the items in the drawing, using the same colour for all the items in a set (e.g. red bowls, blue plates).

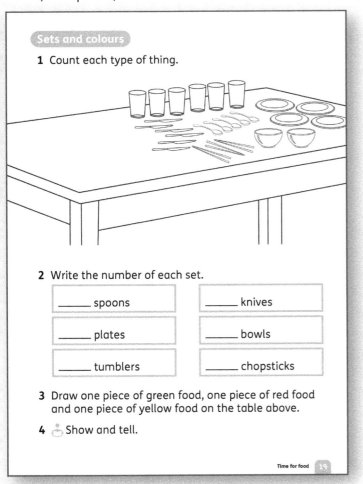

Sets and colours

1 Count each type of thing.

2 Write the number of each set.

_____ spoons	_____ knives
_____ plates	_____ bowls
_____ tumblers	_____ chopsticks

3 Draw one piece of green food, one piece of red food and one piece of yellow food on the table above.

4 🖐 Show and tell.

Time for food 19

In the kitchen

Page 20

Materials needed:

• pencils, colouring materials

Activity teaching notes:

• Warm-up: have a class conversation about kitchens and what children are allowed to do in them.

• Focus on the activity:
  1. Read out the task.
  2. Check that the task is understood.
  3. Ask for oral answers to the first part of the task.
  4. Each learner puts X on dangerous objects and activities.
  5. Remind learners to make the drawing fill the space provided.

• Follow-up – you could use these questions and additional activities.

Let learners show their drawings to one another and explain why the foods are their favourites. Collate the chosen foods on the board and total each one, then ask learners to compare them. Ask: Which is most common? Which is least common?

Ideas for additional activities

Collect data about foods the class dislike. Record the numbers on the board. Then ask learners to make sets (fruits, vegetables, meats, cereals) or to compare numbers of each type.

In the kitchen

1 Name things you can see.

2 Put ☒ on the dangers in the picture.

3 Draw your favourite food. 👩‍🍳 Show and tell.

Learning objectives

- To complete the names of animals and plants
- To measure using squared paper
- To compare lengths and put things in order of length and size
- To sort and count flowers and leaves

Key words

letter, measure, square, count, longest, shape, order, size, smallest, leaves, flowers, colour, set

Topic introduction

- Name of topic: School

- Things to talk about: have a class conversation about learning to read, write and count, encouraging discussion of how learners feel about these new skills.

Time for school

Page 21

Materials needed:

- pencils, colouring materials

Activity teaching notes:

- Warm-up: ask learners one at a time to say the name of something in the room and ask the class to identify the initial letter. Repeat as often as it remains worthwhile.

- Focus on the activity:

  1. Read out the task.
  2. Check that the task is understood.
  3. Individuals should fill in the missing letters for themselves.
  4. The colouring should be done while learners are talking to one another.

- Follow-up – you could use these questions and additional activities.

Ask individuals to share their answers to each word one at a time. Let the class see everyone's coloured pictures.

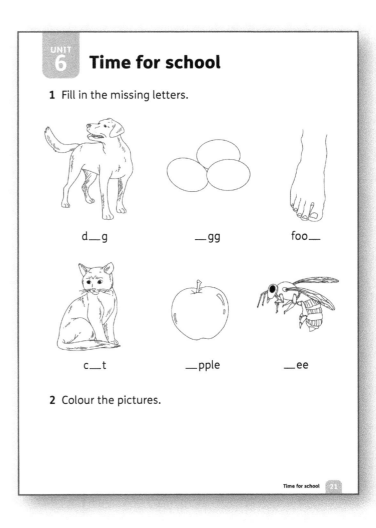

UNIT 6 Time for school

1 Fill in the missing letters.

d__g   __gg   foo__

c__t   __pple   __ee

2 Colour the pictures.

Time for school 21

Ideas for additional activities

Play the 'I-spy' game, with the first item chosen by you and then other items chosen by learners. Individuals should whisper the name of their chosen item to you before the rest of the class begins guessing.

Answers

- Possible answers: missing letters – o, e, t, a, a, b
- Example answers:

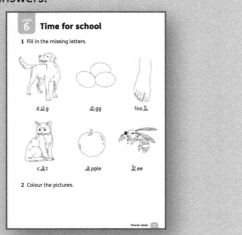

Measuring

Page 22

Materials needed:

- pencils, colouring materials, leaves, crayons

Activity teaching notes:

- Warm-up: get learners to compare the lengths of items in the classroom against their own hands.

- Focus on the activity:

  1. Read out the task.

  2. Check that the task is understood.

  3. Remind learners measure one thing at a time, colouring the squares as they do so.

  4. Once the colouring is completed, the counting of squares should be done and the numbers recorded at the end of each set.

  5. Learners should mark the longest with an X (more than one if two or more are equal length.)

- Follow-up – you could use these questions and additional activities.

Collate the measurements on the board and ask for comments from the class. Encourage them to compare the results, to find the longest and shortest and to order them.

Ideas for additional activities

Invite learners to use interlocking cubes to make 'rulers' and use them to measure items in the room.

Answers

- What drawn answers should include: the number of coloured squares will vary across the class and so will the item marked with X.

Measuring

1 Measure these things using the squares:
   a) hand   **b)** crayon   **c)** leaf   **d)** you choose something.

A

B

C

D

2 Colour the squares for each thing.

3 Count the squares.

4 Which is the longest? Mark it with ☒.

22 Time for school

Shape sets

Page 23

Materials needed:

- pencils, colouring materials

Activity teaching notes:

- Warm-up: lay out a number of objects of the same shape, but different sizes (e.g. marble, tennis ball, football, table tennis ball; pencils of different lengths). Ask learners to sort them in order of size or length.

- Focus on the activity:

  1. Read out the task.

  2. Check that the task is understood.

  3. Remind learners to write 1 on the smallest shape each time.

4. Allow learners to choose which colours to use.

• Follow-up – you could use these questions and additional activities.

Let everyone share their answers by holding up their *Workbooks*. Deal with any differences.

Ideas for additional activities

Repeat the warm-up activity with a larger number of items to sort by size.

Answers

• Possible answers: the numbers from 1 to 4 should be written in the sets of shapes – squares, circles, triangles.

• Example answers:

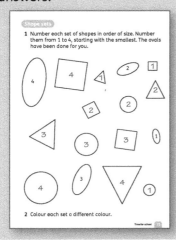

Leaves and flowers

Page 24

Materials needed:

• pencils

Activity teaching notes:

• Warm-up: use blocks or other small items of the same kind but a range of colours for learners to sort into sets based on colour.

• Focus on the activity:

1. Read out the task.

2. Check that the task is understood.

3. Each learner counts and records the numbers in the sets.

• Follow-up – you could use these questions and additional activities.

Let individuals read out their answers and compare them with others in the class. Allow learners to recount their sets where there is disagreement.

Ideas for additional activities

Take learners outside to collect leaves and/or flowers of different colours. On their return to class invite learners to sort them into sets.

Answers

• Possible answers: leaves 10, flowers 10; blue 4, orange 2, white 4, red 2, green 3, yellow 5

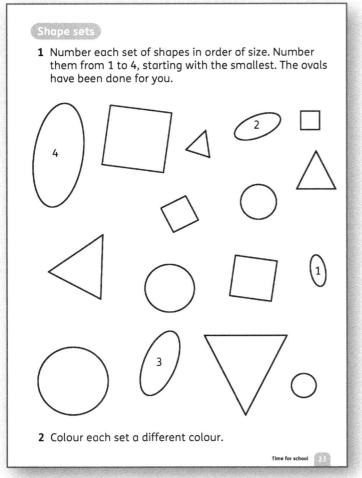

Shape sets

1 Number each set of shapes in order of size. Number them from 1 to 4, starting with the smallest. The ovals have been done for you.

2 Colour each set a different colour.

Time for school 23

Leaves and flowers

1 Count the leaves.

2 Count the flowers.

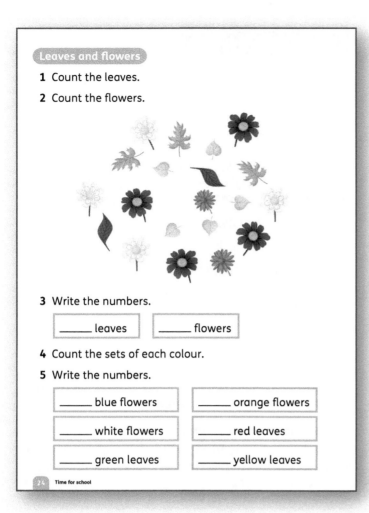

3 Write the numbers.

| _____ leaves | _____ flowers |

4 Count the sets of each colour.

5 Write the numbers.

_____ blue flowers	_____ orange flowers
_____ white flowers	_____ red leaves
_____ green leaves	_____ yellow leaves

UNIT 7 Playtime

Playtime

Page 25

Materials needed:

- pencils, rulers, scissors, pins, square pieces of card, colouring materials

Activity teaching notes:

- Warm-up: ask learners to talk about things that are moved by the wind (e.g. kites, sailing boats, dead leaves, washing on the line, smoke).

- Focus on the activity:

  1. Read out the task.

  2. Check that the task is understood.

  3. Help by cutting the card once the lines have been drawn correctly.

  4. Help pin the four corners together, not too tightly, so the windmill can spin.

  5. When all are ready, go outside and let learners explore how their windmills behave when they wave them around or run with them.

- Follow-up – you could use these questions and additional activities.

Let learners talk about what they saw their windmills do. Encourage them to explain the movement.

UNIT 7 Playtime

1 Follow these steps to make a windmill.

You will need: pencil   ruler   split pin   scissors square piece of card

2 Colour it before you pin it.

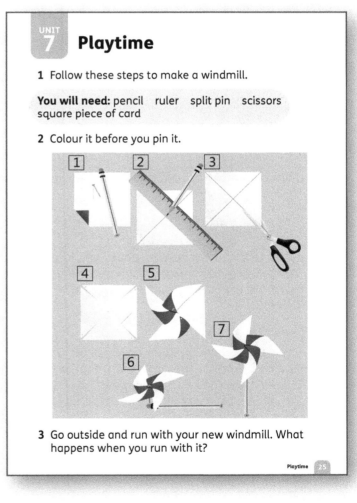

3 Go outside and run with your new windmill. What happens when you run with it?

Playtime 25

Ideas for additional activities

The class can play a game with paper fish shapes with upturned tails. Depending on the space, three or more learners can play at the same time. Each has a piece of thick card and the fish are set out on the floor in front of them. The game is a race. By waving the card up and down, the fish get blown along the floor towards the finishing line.

Answers
- Possible answers: learners should report the spinning of the windmills.

Shapes from blocks

Page 26

Materials needed:

- blocks, pencils, colouring materials

Activity teaching notes:

- Warm-up: have a ready-made shape of five blocks and ask learners to rearrange them into a new shape. Repeat this several times.

- Focus on the activity:

  1. Read out the task.

  2. Check that the task is understood.

  3. Learners play freely with the six blocks, making at least three different shapes.

  4. They choose one shape for their drawing, then colour it in.

  5. Let learners move around and find a drawing different from theirs.

- Follow-up – you could use these questions and additional activities.

Ask everyone to hold up their *Workbooks* and look at the shapes. Ask learners to compare them and if possible find two that are the same. Count the number of different shapes.

Ideas for additional activities

Have a timed task where learners have a short time to make as many shapes as they can, using four or five blocks. It could be turned into a competition. You should record each shape as it is completed so that checking is possible at the end of the time period.

Answers
- What drawn answers should include: a variety of shapes will be drawn, based on what learners make with the blocks. Check that the shapes drawn really are different.

Shapes from blocks

1 Make 3 different shapes from 6 blocks.

2 Draw one of the shapes from blocks. Colour it.

3 Find someone who has a different shape from you.

Play activities

Page 27

Materials needed:

- pencils, colouring materials

Activity teaching notes:

- Warm-up: have a class conversation about what learners do when they play outside, in the school yard, in the garden at home and in the park.

- Focus on the activity:

  1. Read out the task.

  2. Check that the task is understood.

  3. Ask for oral answers to question **1**.

  4. Put learners into pairs or allow them to choose partners. Give the time to examine the picture and talk about their favourite activities.

  5. Individuals draw their own favourite activity.

- Follow-up – you could use these questions and additional activities.

Ask the whole class to hold up their drawings for all to see and encourage comments and questions.

Ideas for additional activities

Take learners outside and encourage them to play in as many ways as the space and equipment allows. Ask them to name the types of play they have chosen.

Answers

- Possible answers: chasing, climbing, sliding, dressing up, role play in the kitchen, sandpit play
- What drawn answers should include: individuals choose their own activity so the drawings will be very varied.

Play activities

1 Name the activities in the picture.

2 Work with a partner. Talk about which two activities you most enjoy.

3 Draw your favourite activity.

Playtime 27

Creative play

Page 28

Materials needed:

- pencils, colouring materials

Activity teaching notes:

Warm-up: hold up a selection of animal pictures and ask learners to say how these animals move.

- Focus on the activity:
  1. Read out the task.
  2. Check that the task is understood.

3. Encourage learners to be as imaginative as possible.

4. The movements should match the drawing as far as possible.

- Follow-up – you could use these questions and additional activities.

The whole class should show their drawings and share their reactions, questions and ideas, with the focus on movement.

Ideas for additional activities

Take learners outside so they can role play the made-up animals, moving around in the ways suggested by the learners.

Answers

- Possible answers: the selection of movements will depend on the imagination of each learner.
- What drawn answers should include: learners are free to draw whatever they can imagine. The only limit is learners' imagination. As the focus is on movement, it should be clear from the drawing how the imaginary animal moves (e.g. by using legs, wings, fins).

Creative play

1 Draw a made-up animal.

2 Colour it.

3 Tick the ways your animal moves:
walk   swim   fly   slide   hop   run

4 Show and tell.

28 Playtime

Learning objectives

- To name objects and identify their textures
- To sort objects related to sleep
- To describe stories and dreams

Key words

sleep, feel, name, story, bedtime, favourite, dream, cross out

Topic introduction

- Name of topic: Sleep
- Things to talk about: have a class conversation about what objects and materials feel like. Introduce descriptive terms such as hard, soft, sticky, flexible, rough, smooth.

Time for sleep

Page 29

Materials needed:

- pencils

Activity teaching notes:

- Warm-up: ask learners to talk about bedtime.
- Focus on the activity:
  1. Read out the task.
  2. Check that the task is understood.
  3. Ask for oral answers to question **1**.
  4. Learners should each add X marks on the things they think are hard and circle the things they think are soft.
- Follow-up – you could use these questions and additional activities.

Collate a list of hard items and soft items on the board. Add them up and ask learners to comment.

UNIT 8 Time for sleep

1 Name the things you see.

2 Put X on the hard things. Circle the soft things.

Time for sleep 29

Ideas for additional activities

Ask learners to look around the room and find soft and hard items. Make a collection of some items and mix them together. Then ask individual learners to sort them into two sets. Introduce other items chosen by yourself and ask learners to put them in the correct set.

> **Answers**
> - Possible answers: door, table, desk, bookcase, books, screen, computer keyboard, beds, basket, pillows, sheets, teddy bear, fan, hat, pictures, shelf, children, mat, window, lamp
> - What drawn answers should include: X on most things listed above; circles around pillows, sheets, teddy bear, mattresses on beds, clothes

Sleeping places

Page 30

Materials needed:

- pencils

Activity teaching notes:

- Warm-up: have a class conversation about sleeping
- Focus on the activity:
  1. Read out the task.
  2. Check that the task is understood.
  3. Learners will mark animals with a X if they have seen them.
  4. Have a class conversation for learners to answer the two questions about when and where they sleep.
- Follow-up – you could use these questions and additional activities.

Ask learners to explain when they saw the animals they marked with an X.

Ideas for additional activities

Ask learners to mime falling asleep: from the first drowsy feelings to being fully asleep. If possible, do the activity in a space where all the learners can 'fall asleep' on the floor.

> **Answers**
> - Possible answers: the answers will depend on which animals have been seen (e.g. a cat curled up in front of a fire, a hamster asleep in its 'nest' of soft material).

Sleeping places

1 Put a ☒ by any animal you have seen.

2 When do you sleep? Where do you sleep?

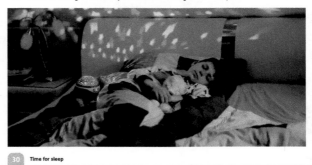

Sleep time

Page 31

Materials needed:

- pencils, colouring materials

Activity teaching notes:

- Warm-up: ask learners to name anything they think of when you say 'bedtime'.
- Focus on the activity:
  1. Read out the task.
  2. Check that the task is understood.
  3. Make sure that the crossing out happens before the colouring.
- Follow-up – you could use these questions and additional activities.

Collate the answers on the board. Discuss any disagreements about the crossed out items.

Ideas for additional activities

Ask learners to mime waking up. If possible, start with the class lying down on the floor 'asleep'. They will need enough space between them to allow the movements of waking up.

Answers

- Possible answers: crossed out items – table, bicycle, umbrella, sun, hat, school clothes, coat
- Example answers:

- Focus on the activity:

1. Read out the task.

2. Check that the task is understood.

3. Have a class conversation about the two questions at the top of the page.

4. Individuals are free to draw whatever they choose.

- Follow-up – you could use these questions and additional activities.

Let all learners show their dream pictures and encourage them to ask questions and describe the content of the dreams.

Ideas for additional activities

Encourage learners to talk about the feelings associated with their dreams.

Answers

- Possible answers: learners' answers will vary.
- What drawn answers should include: individuals do their own drawings, so the pictures will be very varied. As dreams are imaginary, there is no limit to what the pictures may contain.

Sleep time

1 Cross out the things which have nothing to do with sleep time.

2 Colour the sleep items.

Time for sleep 31

Page 32

Materials needed:

- pencils, colouring materials

Activity teaching notes:

- Warm-up: ask learners to talk about the Moon, with particular focus on when it is seen.

UNIT 9 Special days

Learning objectives

- To identify and name objects
- To sort items
- To describe events and experiences
- To identify movements and activities
- To identify and continue patterns

Key words

special, wedding, party, birthday, cross out, procession, carnival, flags, costume, moving, pattern, order, size, line, number, playing, dancing, clapping, singing, smiling

Topic introduction

- Name of topic: Special days
- Things to talk about: have a class conversation about any special days the learners can remember.

Special days

Page 33

Materials needed:

- pencils

Activity teaching notes:

- Warm-up: ask learners to share their experiences of birthday parties.
- Focus on the activity:
  1. Read out the task.
  2. Check that the task is understood.
  3. Let learners cross out the items they think are not found at birthday parties.
  4. They can mark items they like best with a tick and a X for those they would not like at the party.
- Follow-up – you could use these questions and additional activities.

Collate the items on the board with one list for the most liked items and one list for the least liked items. Total each one and ask learners to identify the most and the least liked items. Discuss why they have been chosen.

UNIT 9 **Special days**

1 Cross out all the things you do **not** see on the table at a party.

2 Put ☑ on the thing you like best. Put ☒ on the thing you would not like at your party.

Special days 33

Ideas for additional activities

Invite learners to make up a 'dream menu' composed of all the favourite foods for a birthday party.

> **Answers**
> - Possible answers: crossed out – fish, shoe, cabbage/lettuce, whole carrots, toothbrush
> - What drawn answers should include: ticks and crosses will be put on various items depending on learners' choices.

A wedding

Page 34

Materials needed:

- pencils

Activity teaching notes:

- Warm-up: let learners tell one another about weddings they have attended.
- Focus on the activity:
  1. Read out the task.
  2. Check that the task is understood.
  3. Put the learners into pairs or allow them to find partners. Focus their attention on what is shown in the picture.
  4. Individuals should draw their own lines from words to the correct parts of the picture.
- Follow-up – you could use these questions and additional activities.

Ask learners to share their answers and deal with any disagreements.

Ideas for additional activities

Use class musical instruments to have a 'wedding dance', where some play the music and others do the dancing. The roles can then be swapped.

Answers

- What drawn answers should include: lines from word boxes to the actions in the picture.
- Example answers:

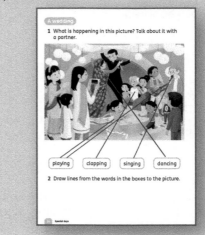

A wedding

1 What is happening in this picture? Talk about it with a partner.

playing   clapping   singing   dancing

2 Draw lines from the words in the boxes to the picture.

A fair

Page 35

Materials needed:

- pencils

Activity teaching notes:

- Warm-up: let learners share their experiences of fairgrounds.
- Focus on the activity:
  1. Read out the task.
  2. Check that the task is understood.
  3. Individuals should look at the picture and choose the activity to circle as their favourite.
  4. Word boxes should be linked to the correct parts of the picture.
- Follow-up – you could use these questions and additional activities.

Collate on the board the list of favourite activities. Ask learners to total each item and then identify the most and the least popular.

Ideas for additional activities

Take learners outside and ask them to move in the three ways listed on the page – round and round; up and down; up and down and round and round at the same time.

A fair
1 What would you like to do at the fair? Circle your favourite thing.
round and round
up and down
up and down and round and round
2 Draw lines from the words in the boxes to the picture.
Special days 35

Answers

- Possible answers: the answers will be varied as each learner is free to choose.
- What drawn answers should include: the lines should link
  - round and round to teacups ride
  - up and down to water slide
  - roller coaster to up and down
  - round and round to the roundabout and the big wheel.

A carnival

Page 36

Materials needed:

- pencils

Activity teaching notes:

- Warm-up: have a class conversation about carnivals.
- Focus on the activity:
  1. Read out the task.
  2. Check that the task is understood.
  3. Learners use X to mark moving things.
  4. The pattern of flags is continued in the space below the picture. Remind learners to fill the space.
- Follow-up – you could use these questions and additional activities.

Collate the list of moving things and total the answers for each one. Ask learners to find the one chosen most often and the one chosen least often.

Ideas for additional activities

Take the class outside and have a carnival march, with musical instruments, waving and shouting.

Answers

- Possible answers: moving things – arms, people marching, balloons, flags, drummer, floats, fingers of musicians
- What drawn answers should include: the pattern should be triangles of blue and yellow repeated as often as the space allows.

A carnival

1 Mark the moving things with a ☒.

2 Look for the pattern in the little flags. Continue the pattern.

• What drawn answers should include: individuals draw their own costume so the drawings will be very varied. Costumes should be colourful, unusual or even strange. If possible, costumes can have masks.

3 Draw a costume you would wear to a carnival. Show and tell.

Page 37

Materials needed:

• pencils, colouring materials

Activity teaching notes:

• Warm-up: allow some learners to use items from the dressing-up box and let the class see and comment on them.

• Focus on the activity:

1. Read out the task.

2. Check that the task is understood.

3. Remind learners to fill the space provided and make the costume colourful.

• Follow-up – you could use these questions and additional activities.

Let the whole class show their drawings. Ask questions to encourage discussion about how suitable the costumes are for a carnival parade.

Ideas for additional activities

Invite learners to use the dressing-up box to find some clothes most suited to a carnival parade.

UNIT
10 Growing

Growing

Page 38

Materials needed:

- pencils

Activity teaching notes:

- Warm-up: ask learners to identify things they cannot do at the moment, especially things connected with height and strength.

- Focus on the activity:

  1. Read out the task.

  2. Check that the task is understood.

  3. Individuals should add A and B to the pictures to sort them into two sets.

  4. Check that they write 1 for the youngest in each set.

- Follow-up – you could use these questions and additional activities.

Ask learners to identify some of the signs of growth shown in the pictures.

Ideas for additional activities

Make sets of cards or pictures showing stages in the life of other animals and ask learners to sort them in order of age. Ask them to explain how they decided the order.

Answers

- Possible answers: (A) by baby, boy and man; (B) by egg, chick and hen

UNIT 10 Growing

1 Look at the pictures. Put A by the pictures of people. Put B by the pictures that are **not** people.

2 Put each set in order of age. Write (1) (2) or (3) beside them. 1 should be the youngest, 3 the oldest.

38 Growing

Height

Page 39

Materials needed:

• pencils, colouring materials

Activity teaching notes:

• Warm-up: ask learners to look around the room and compare the heights of things around them, finding the tallest thing in the room.

• Focus on the activity:

1. Read out the task.

2. Check that the task is understood.

3. Remind learners to write 1 for the shortest person.

4. Remind learners to fill as much space as they can with their drawing.

• Follow-up – you could use these questions and additional activities.

Let learners show their drawings and talk about them.

Ideas for additional activities

Ask learners to arrange themselves in order of height. Then have a conversation about age. Do height and age always increase together?

Wheels

Page 40

Materials needed:

• pencils, colouring materials

Activity teaching notes:

• Warm-up: look at the pictures with the class and ask why the machines have different numbers of wheels and are different sizes.

• Focus on the activity:

1. Read out the task.

2. Check that the task is understood.

3. Ask for oral answers to the question **1**.

4. Put learners into pairs or let them choose partners.

5. Allow learners time to explain why they would prefer to ride one bike or trike than the others.

• Follow-up – you could use these questions and additional activities.

Let the class look at one another's coloured pictures. Collate the choices on the board, total them and have a discussion of why there are more who chose one thing than the others. Focus on the issue of size and having the ability to balance on two-wheeled machines.

Ideas for additional activities

Take learners outside and let them use the wheeled toys. Talk about how the toys work.

Height

1 Put the family in order of height.

2 Write 1–5 beside each family member. 1 is the shortest, 5 is the tallest.

3 Draw yourself and a family member who is taller than you.

Growing 39

Wheels

1 How many wheels can you see on this page?
Point and add.

2 Work with a partner. Talk about which picture you
would like to ride on.

3 Colour the pictures.

Seeds

Teaching guidance

Page 41

Materials needed:

- beans, jars or clear plastic pots, water, kitchen roll,
pencils

Activity teaching notes:

- Warm-up: let learners share their experiences of the
growth of seeds.

- Focus on the activity:

1. Read out the task.

2. Check that the task is understood.

3. This practical task will need adult help, so you may
need to do it a group at a time, depending on how
many adults you have available.

4. Let learners do as much for themselves as you can.

5. Put the jars aside in a safe place where learners
can look at them each day to check the changes in
the seeds.

6. The drawing can be from imagination or a picture
of what the grown seeds produce.

- Follow-up – you could use these questions and
additional activities.

Once the whole activity is completed, ask learners to
show their drawings to one another and talk about the
changes that have taken place since the seeds were put
in the jars.

Ideas for additional activities

The class can sow other seeds on pieces of wet kitchen
roll or fabric, on saucers or shallow dishes. The seeds will
need to be kept watered enough to prevent them drying
out. Ask learners to compare the growth of these seeds
with the seeds they grew in jars.

Answers

- What drawn answers should include: a plant with
leaves, stem and roots should be drawn from
imagination or from life.

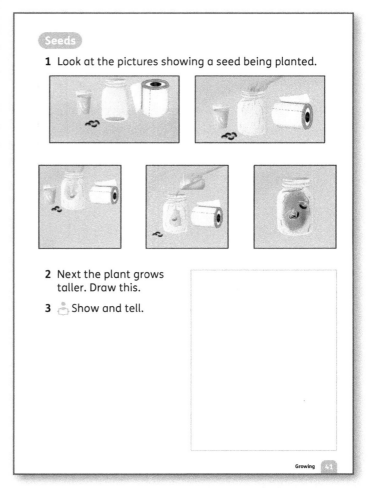

Seeds

1 Look at the pictures showing a seed being planted.

2 Next the plant grows
taller. Draw this.

3 Show and tell.

Growing   41

UNIT 11 Changes

Learning objectives

- To identify pulls and pushes
- To identify the stages in a bird's life
- To be able to sow seeds and know what they need to germinate

Key words

class, pull, push, story, bird, adult, eggs, finish, make up, seed, soil, water, plant, leaves

Topic introduction

- Name of topic: Changes
- Things to talk about: have a class conversation about things that change – such as the sky, the weather, the time of day, the date.

Changes

Page 42

Materials needed:

- pencils, colouring materials

Activity teaching notes:

- Warm-up: continue the conversation about changes but focus on plants and animals.
- Focus on the activity:
  1. Read out the task.
  2. Check that the task is understood.
  3. Ask individuals to tell the story of the bird, moving from one learner to another until the end.
  4. Learners should put the tick on the bird they choose.
  5. Remind them to use all the space given for drawing.
- Follow-up – you could use these questions and additional activities.

Learners look at each other's drawings. Collate the colours on the board and total them. Ask learners to put the colours in order of frequency, from least common to most common.

Ideas for additional activities

Make a set of pictures showing the stages of an insect life cycle. Randomly arrange them and ask learners to put them in the correct order.

Answers

- Possible answers: the bird on the right is the adult.
- What drawn answers should include: these will vary as each learner is free to choose.

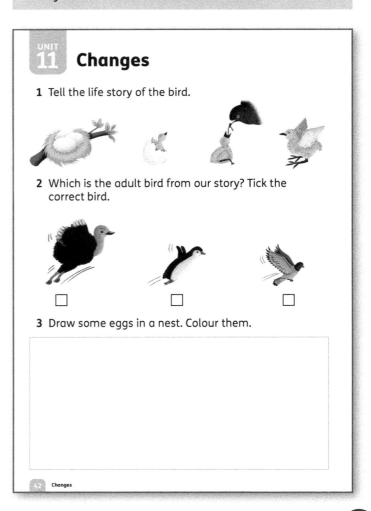

UNIT 11 Changes

1 Tell the life story of the bird.

2 Which is the adult bird from our story? Tick the correct bird.

☐   ☐   ☐

3 Draw some eggs in a nest. Colour them.

42 Changes

Growing and changing

Page 43

Materials needed:

• pencils

Activity teaching notes:

• Warm-up: have a conversation about growing plants from seeds.

• Focus on the activity:

1. Read out the task.

2. Check that the task is understood.

3. Each learner should enter the numbers in the boxes.

• Follow-up – you could use these questions and additional activities.

Compare learners' answers and deal with any disagreements. Ask learners to explain why they put the stages in the order they did.

Ideas for additional activities

Learners sow seeds of various kinds in pots of soil and compare how they grow and develop.

Answers

• Possible answers: order is 4, 1, 3, 2

• Example answers:

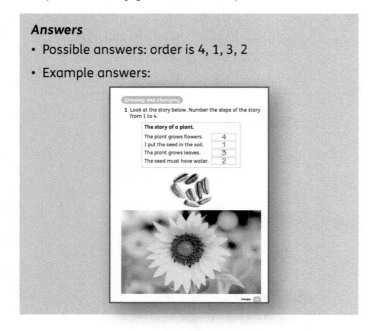

1 Look at the story below. Number the steps of the story from 1 to 4.

The story of a plant.	
The plant grows flowers.	
I put the seed in the soil.	
The plant grows leaves.	
The seed must have water.	

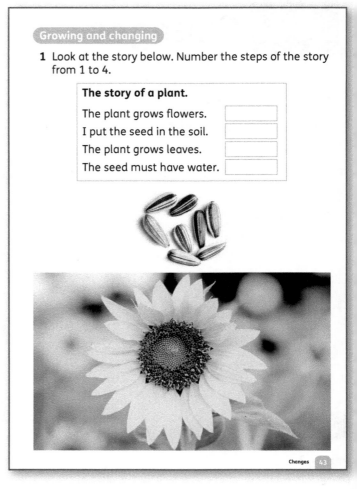

Changes 43

Push and pull

Page 44

Materials needed:

• pencils

Activity teaching notes:

• Warm-up: ask learners to use their hands to pull objects towards them and then to push objects away from them.

• Focus on the activity:

1. Read out the task.

2. Check that the task is understood.

3. Each learner copies the words 'push' and 'pull' to answer the six questions on the page.

• Follow-up – you could use these questions and additional activities.

Ask learners to give oral answers to the six questions. Deal with any disagreements.

Ideas for additional activities

Go outside with learners and use the toys and equipment to demonstrate pushes and pulls.

Answers

- Possible answers: push, pull, push, pull, pull, push
- Example answers:

- Focus on the activity:
  1. Read out the task.
  2. Check that the task is understood.
  3. Allow learners to move around and find things to pull. The drawing of one object should be done before finding objects to push. Each learner then chooses one of the pushed objects to draw.

- Follow-up – you could use these questions and additional activities.

Learners look at all the drawings and talk about the objects shown. Ask how easy or difficult it was to move things. Focus on things with and without wheels.

Ideas for additional activities

Invite learners to make a model of something that can be pulled.

Answers

- What drawn answers should include: each learner is free to choose objects so the drawings will be very varied. Allow any drawings of pushed objects, even if some are not wheeled or normally pushed (e.g. a box, a chair or a pillow).

Push and pull

1 Write the correct word: push or pull.

_____ _____

_____ _____

_____ _____

44 Changes

---

2 Find some things in the classroom. Try pulling them. Draw one of them.

3 Find some things in the classroom. Try pushing them. Draw one of them.

Changes 45

Page 45

Materials needed:

- pencils, toys and other objects to push and/or pull

Activity teaching notes:

- Warm-up: ask learners to talk about their experiences of pulling and pushing things, especially heavy things without or with wheels.

Plants

Learning objectives

- To arrange items in order of size
- To know that leaves, seeds, flowers and fruits vary in size, shape and colour
- To identify and name seeds, flowers and fruits

Key words

plant, leaf, collect, order, size, seed, pea, bean, cashew, sunflower, rice, count, red, blue, yellow, flower, shape, fruit, orange, banana, strawberry, melon, apple, mango, tomato

Topic introduction

- Name of topic: Plants
- Things to talk about: have a class conversation about plants – what learners know about them, particularly their parts.

Plants

Page 2

Materials needed:

- pencils, colouring materials leaves

Activity teaching notes:

- Warm-up: show learners a variety of leaves from indoor and outdoor plants and ask them to describe them, comparing colours, shapes, sizes, etc.
- Focus on the activity:
  1. Read out the task.
  2. Check that the task is understood.
  3. Each learner does the counting and recording step independently.
  4. Let learners go out to collect three different leaves if possible. Alternatively, have a selection of more than three leaf types for them to choose from. Remind learners to use all the space available for their drawing.
- Follow-up – you could use these questions and additional activities.

Let learners show their drawings to one another and compare them. Ask them to focus on size differences, but note shape and colour too.

Ideas for additional activities

Use leaves with prominent veins to make leaf rubbings; using wax crayons and sheets of blank writing paper.

Answers

- Possible answers: 5, 3, 2, 4
- What drawn answers should include: the drawings will all vary as the leaves are chosen by learners.

UNIT
1
Plants

1 Count each type of leaf. Write the numbers in the blanks.

_____   _____   _____   _____

2 Collect 3 different leaves.

3 Put your leaves in order of size, smallest to largest.

4 Draw them in order of size.

2 Plants

Seeds and flowers

Page 3

Materials needed:

- pencils, colouring materials

Activity teaching notes:

- Warm-up: show a variety of well-known and less common seeds to the class and ask them to talk about them, comparing sizes, shapes, colours, etc. Include the four seed types illustrated on the page.

- Focus on the activity:

  1. Read out the task.

  2. Check that the task is understood.

  3. Each learner draws lines from pictures to names.

  4. The colouring of the flowers is for each learner to choose.

- Follow-up – you could use these questions and additional activities.

Show again the mixed seeds you used in the warm-up. Ask learners to pick out the four types shown in the pictures.

Ideas for additional activities

Invite learners to sort the mixed seeds using different criteria (e.g. colour, size, shape).

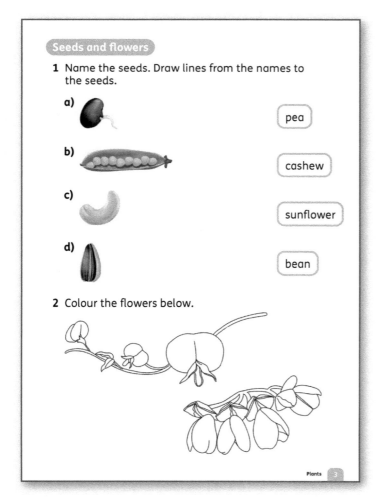

Pages 4–5

Materials needed:

- pencils, colouring materials, flowers

Activity teaching notes:

- Warm-up: use a bunch of real flowers or picture of mixed flowers to start a class conversation about the variety of flowers – shape, colour, size, scent, etc.

- Focus on the activity:

  1. Read out the task.

  2. Check that the task is understood.

  3. The counting and recording should be done individually.

  4. Comparing the shapes leads to drawing and colouring two different ones.

  5. Let the class see the drawings and talk about them.

- Follow-up – you could use these additional activities.

Ask learners to talk about their favourite flower colours and explain why these are their favourites.

Ideas for additional activities

Turn the data about the flowers on the page into a class-made block graph, using either interlocking blocks or large squared paper for learners to colour in the correct number of squares for each of the six flower types.

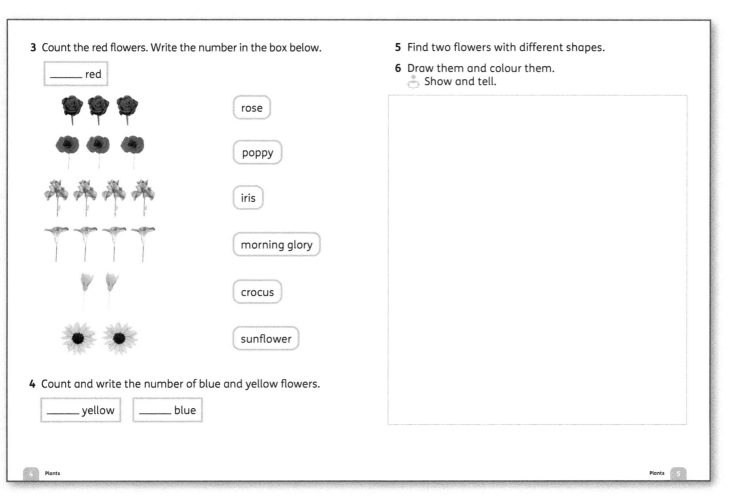

3 Count the red flowers. Write the number in the box below.

_____ red

rose

poppy

iris

morning glory

crocus

sunflower

4 Count and write the number of blue and yellow flowers.

_____ yellow   _____ blue

5 Find two flowers with different shapes.

6 Draw them and colour them.
   Show and tell.

Fruits

Page 6

Materials needed:

• pencils, colouring materials

Activity teaching notes:

• Warm-up: have a class conversation about eating fruits and encourage learners to say why they like some fruits more than others.

• Focus on the activity:

  1. Read out the task.

  2. Check that the task is understood.

  3. The colouring should be finished before the lines are drawn connecting names to fruits.

  4. Learners should freely choose which flowers and fruits to draw.

• Follow-up – you could use these questions and additional activities.

Let learners see one another's drawings, ask questions and make comments about what has been drawn.

Ideas for additional activities

Cut a number of fruits in half crossways to reveal the seed chambers and seeds. Encourage learners to talk about what they see and what they understand about the relationship between fruits and seeds (e.g. orange, tomato, melon, apple, mango).

Answers

• Possible answers: lines connect fruits to the names orange, banana, strawberry, apple.

• What drawn answers should include: individuals choose their own flowers and fruits so the drawings will be very varied.

Fruits

1 Colour the fruits.

2 Name the fruits. Draw lines from the names to the fruits.

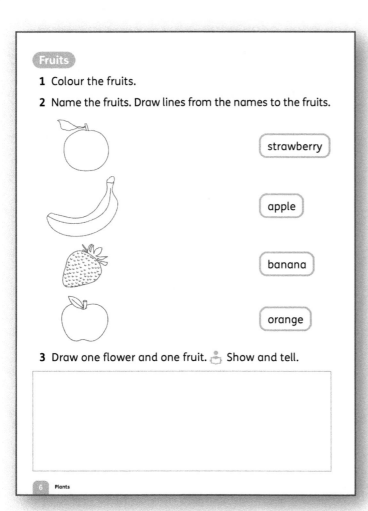

strawberry

apple

banana

orange

3 Draw one flower and one fruit. Show and tell.

6 Plants

UNIT 2 Animals

Learning objectives

- To identify and name some animals
- To know that each animal fits its environment
- To identify animal movements
- To complete animal drawings

Key words

animal, adult, young, bird, count, dog, cat, sheep, horse, penguin, hen, legs, walk, swim, fly, slide, move, desert, Arctic, jungle, sea, grassland, place

Topic introduction

- Name of topic: Animals
- Things to talk about: have a class conversation about animals, drawing on learners' experience of pets, zoos, holidays, open spaces including parks.

Animals

Page 7

Materials needed:

- pencils, colouring materials

Activity teaching notes:

- Warm-up: have pictures of two animals that have very different adults and young (e.g. tadpole and frog; caterpillar and butterfly). Ask learners to talk about them and find out whether anyone knows that they show young and adult stages.

- Focus on the activity:

  1. Read out the task.

  2. Check that the task is understood.

  3. Do step 2 first, asking for oral answers to identify the animals.

  4. The lines linking adults and babies should be done individually, followed by ticking the birds.

  5. The number of legs should be written on the lines under the pictures.

- Follow-up – you could use these questions and additional activities.

Ask learners to name the babies shown in the pictures.

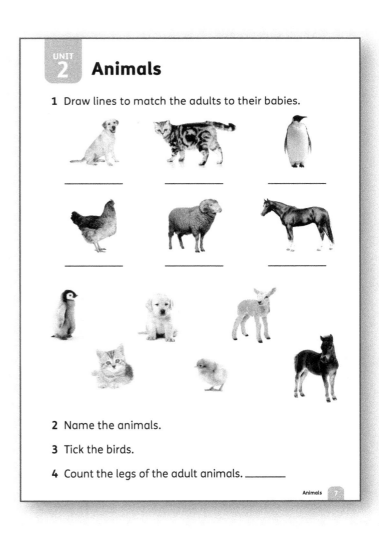

UNIT 2 Animals

1 Draw lines to match the adults to their babies.

2 Name the animals.

3 Tick the birds.

4 Count the legs of the adult animals. _____

Animals 7

Ideas for additional activities

On the board, make a list of animals given to you by the class then ask them to sort them into sets based on the number of legs each has. Encourage them to think of birds, fish, insects and legless land and sea creatures, as well as four-legged land mammals. Total each set and sort the sets by order of size.

Answers

- Possible answers: learners should name the animals: (dog, cat, sheep, horse) and tick the birds: (penguin, hen). The animals each have four legs.

Animal colours

Page 8

Materials needed:

- pencils, colouring materials

Activity teaching notes:

- Warm-up: have a class conversation about brightly coloured and patterned animals.

- Focus on the activity:

  1. Read out the task.

  2. Check that the task is understood.

  3. After the colouring is finished, ask for the names of the animals as oral answers.

  4. The numbers of legs should be written on the lines under the animals.

- Follow-up – you could use these additional activities.

Let everyone share their completed pictures. Compare, comment on and question what learners have done.

Ideas for additional activities

Show pictures of animals that camouflage themselves with their colours and patterns (e.g. tiger, octopus, plaice, chameleon). Have a class discussion about the colours and patterns to find out how much learners understand about these being useful in keeping animals safe and hiding from predators.

Answers

- Possible answers: zebra 4, parrot 2, butterfly 6.

- What drawn answers should include: the completed drawings will be very varied.

Animal colours

1 Finish colouring the animals.

_____

_____

_____

2 Name the animals.

3 Count the legs. Write the numbers.

4 🎨 Show and tell.

8 Animals

Animal movement

Page 9

Materials needed:

- pencils

Activity teaching notes:

- Warm-up: let learners mime the movements of animals, without telling the class which animals they are miming. Ask the class to identify the animals.

- Focus on the activity:

  1. Read out the task.

  2. Check that the task is understood.

  3. Ask for oral answers naming the animals.

  4. The number of legs should be written under the pictures.

  5. Some animals can move in more than one way, so remind learners of this when they are drawing the lines.

- Follow-up – you could use these questions and additional activities.

Ask learners to identify any of the animals that can move in two or more ways.

Ideas for additional activities

Collate on the board a list of animals that move in various ways. Ask learners to number the ways each one can move from 1 to 4. Sort them into sets based on the number of ways they move. Use the data to create a block graph, either made of interlocking cubes or on large squared paper, on which learners colour the correct numbers of squares.

Answers

- Possible answers: penguin 2 swim, walk; duck 2 swim, walk, fly; snake 0 slide; snail 0 slide; giraffe 4 walk; shark 0 swim.
- Example answers:

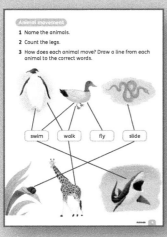

Animal places

Page 10

Materials needed:

- pencils

Activity teaching notes:

- Warm-up: have a class conversation about the various places where animals live (e.g. in trees, in the sea, under the ground).
- Focus on the activity:
  1. Read out the task.
  2. Check that the task is understood.
  3. Each learner draws the four lines to connect animals to their places.
  4. The names of the places should then be connected to the pictures with lines.
  5. Have a class conversation about what other animals live in each place. Collate the names on the board.
- Follow-up – you could use these questions and additional activities.

Invite learners to look at the lists of animals for each place. Ask them to find common features for each set (e.g. Arctic animals are fat or furry; sea animals have fins or flippers; jungle animals have climbing arms and legs; grassland animals can run).

Ideas for additional activities

Make a display of the four places: copy the page of the book, cut it into the four parts, add the names to each part and ask learners to draw some of the other animals that live in each place. Cut these out and arrange them around the appropriate places in the display.

Answers

- Possible answers: deer, grassland; octopus, sea; polar bear, Arctic; gorilla, jungle.

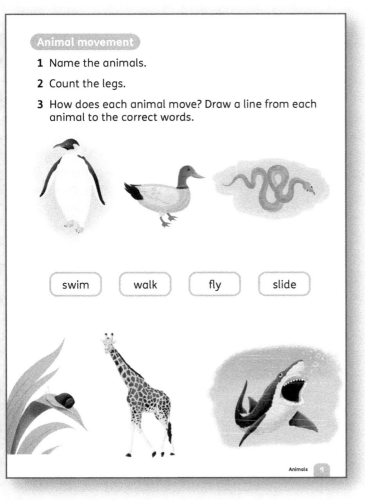

Animal places

1 Match the animals to where they live. Draw lines from the animals to the places.

2 Match the words to the places. Draw lines.

(sea)   (jungle)   (grassland)   (Arctic)

3 What other animals live in each place?

 Animals

UNIT 3 Weather

Learning objectives

- To identify and name some weather elements
- To know that the weather affects what we wear
- To identify various weather conditions
- To know that we use the wind in various ways
- To understand that rain and snow return water to the streams, rivers, etc.

Key words

weather, lightning, cloud, sun, hail, snow, wind, rain, wet, hot, cold, clothes, cross out, fan, move, drop, pond, stream, river, lake, sea, snowy, mountain, glacier, ice cap, iceberg

Topic introduction

- Name of topic: The weather
- Things to talk about: have a class discussion about the weather, the way it changes and how we feel about different types of weather. Ask: Does the weather stay the same all day? How do you feel about very hot weather?

Weather

Page 11

Materials needed:

- pencils, colouring materials

Activity teaching notes:

- Warm-up: let learners mime aspects of the weather and how they make us feel.

- Focus on the activity:

  1. Read out the task.
  2. Check that the task is understood.
  3. Learners draw lines to link words and symbols.
  4. Learners look at the weather then choose weather symbols to draw. Words should be added to the symbols.

- Follow-up – you could use these questions and additional activities.

Ask learners to report to the class which symbols they used for the day's weather and deal with any disagreements.

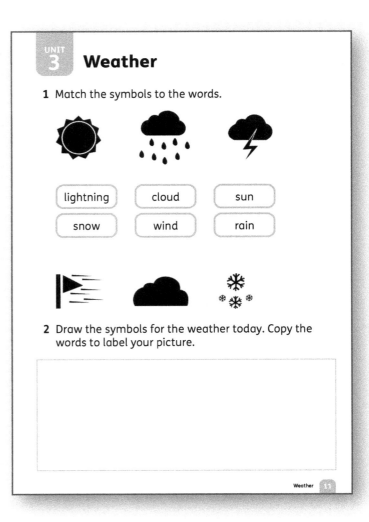

UNIT 3 Weather

1 Match the symbols to the words.

lightning   cloud   sun

snow   wind   rain

2 Draw the symbols for the weather today. Copy the words to label your picture.

Weather 11

Ideas for additional activities

Make one set of cards with the names and another with the symbols. Play a matching game where players try to find the pairs: word + symbol. Place all cards with either the words or the symbols on show.

A player takes one card then turns over another card, hoping it forms a pair with the first. If it does, they keep the cards. Each player in turn tries to find pairs.

Answers

- Possible answers: sun, rain, lightning, wind, cloud, snow
- What drawn answers should include: the drawings will vary as each learner chooses symbols.

Weather and clothes

Page 12

Materials needed:

- pencils, colouring materials

Activity teaching notes:

- Warm-up: have a class conversation about what clothes have to be like for different types of weather (e.g. thick, waterproof, thin, heavy, light).

- Focus on the activity:

  1. Read out the task.
  2. Check that the task is understood.
  3. Ask for oral answers for the names of the clothes shown in the drawings.
  4. Each learner should trace the words for the three sets of clothes.
  5. Allow learners total freedom to choose the type of clothing for a wet or cold day.

- Follow-up – you could use these questions and additional activities.

Ask learners to show their drawings to the class and get them to identify the type of weather each one is for. Deal with any disagreements.

Ideas for additional activities

Ask learners to mime how they move on windy days.

Answers

- Possible answers: cold, wet, hot
- What drawn answers should include: the drawings will be very varied but should match one of the two weather types – wet or cold.

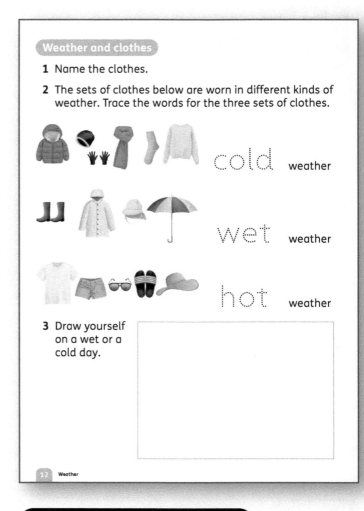

Weather and clothes

1 Name the clothes.

2 The sets of clothes below are worn in different kinds of weather. Trace the words for the three sets of clothes.

cold weather

wet weather

hot weather

3 Draw yourself on a wet or a cold day.

12 Weather

Things which use the wind

Page 13

Materials needed:

- pencils, paper, elastic bands

Activity teaching notes:

- Warm-up: have a class conversation about how we can tell it is windy – by seeing things, hearing things, feeling things.

- Focus on the activity:

  1. Read out the task.
  2. Check that the task is understood.
  3. Individual learners cross out the items that do not use the wind.

Ideas for additional activities

Invite learners to make simple paper airplanes and take them outside to fly them.

Answers

- Possible answers: crossed out – car, train, rocket, girl drinking

Things which use the wind

1 Cross out the things which do not use the wind.

Weather 13

Types of weather

Page 14

Materials needed:

- pencils

Activity teaching notes:

- Warm-up: ask about rain, hail, clouds and snow and see whether learners make any connections between them as different forms of water.

- Focus on the activity:

  1. Read out the task.

  2. Check that the task is understood.

  3. The rain drops should be added to the three pictures at the top of the page.

  4. The snowflakes should be drawn on the two lower pictures.

- Follow-up – you could use these questions and additional activities.

Have a class conversation about what keeps rivers, lakes and the sea 'filled' with water. Focus on the connection between rainfall and water on the surface of the Earth.

Ideas for additional activities

Invite learners to watch ice cubes change as they are kept in the classroom on a dish. Encourage learners to use the correct terms when talking about their observations – ice, frozen, solid, melting, liquid, water.

Answers

- What drawn answers should include: simple representations of rain and snow should be added to the relevant pictures.

Types of weather

1 It's raining. Add rain drops to each picture.

river   lake   sea

2 It's snowing. Add snowflakes to each picture.

snow mountains

iceberg

14 Weather

Page 15

Materials needed:

• pencils, colouring materials

Activity teaching notes:

• Warm-up: recap on the conversations about how weather changes how we feel, especially the weather that make us feel positive, happy, good.

• Focus on the activity.

  1. Read out the task.

  2. Check that the task is understood.

  3. Remind learners to use the whole space for their drawings. Each one can choose their favourite weather.

• Follow-up – you could use these questions and additional activities.

Let the class see one another's drawings and encourage them to ask questions about why these types of weather are the favourites.

Ideas for additional activities

Have a class conversation about the most disliked weather. Ask learners for their reasons for disliking it.

> **Answers**
> • What drawn answers should include: each drawing will depend on learners' choice. The weather features that learners choose should be clear (e.g. heavy rain, bright sunshine or snowfall).

3 Draw your favourite type of weather.
  Show and tell.

Weather 15

Learning objectives

- To know that some living things live in the soil
- To know that we eat some roots
- To know that seeds need certain things to grow

Key words

soil, animal, underground, cross out, touch, home, roots, eat, plant, sweet potato, carrot, radish, beetroot, seed

Topic introduction

- Name of topic: Soil
- Things to talk about: have a class conversation about what soil is and where it is found and how it is used by people.

 Soil

Page 16

Materials needed:

- pencils, colouring materials

Activity teaching notes:

- Warm-up: have a conversation about what life underground would be like for people. Encourage learners to use their imagination when answering.

- Focus on the activity:

  1. Read out the task.

  2. Check that the task is understood.

  3. Ask for oral answers to name the animals.

  4. Each learner crosses out animals that do not live in the soil.

  5. The drawing is an opportunity for learners to use their imagination.

- Follow-up – you could use these questions and additional activities.

The class should all share their drawings, ask questions and compare the ideas they introduce.

Ideas for additional activities

Learners can mime different animals digging their homes in soil.

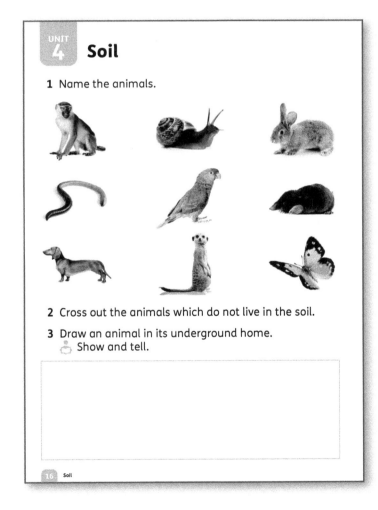

Roots

Page 17

Materials needed:

- pencils, colouring materials

Activity teaching notes:

- Warm-up: have a class conversation about the vegetables learners eat, identifying which part of the plant each vegetable is.
- Focus on the activity:

  1. Read out the task.
  2. Check that the task is understood.
  3. Ask learners to connect the incomplete plants to their names in the boxes.
  4. The roots should be completed in the correct colours and size.

- Follow-up – you could use these questions and additional activities.

Ask the class to share their drawings and compare the shapes of the roots.

Ideas for additional activities

Read together a storybook such as *Plant the Tiny Seed* by Christie Matheson, *The Ugly Vegetables* by Grace Lin or *The Enormous Turnip* by Irene Yates. Then act out the story.

Answers

- What drawn answers should include: the drawings should be in scale, the correct colour and shape.

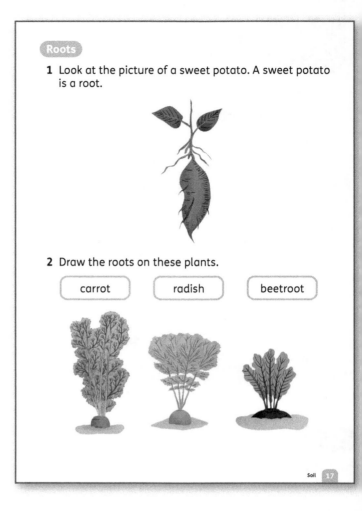

Roots

1 Look at the picture of a sweet potato. A sweet potato is a root.

2 Draw the roots on these plants.

carrot   radish   beetroot

Soil 17

What seeds need

Page 18

Materials needed:

- pencils, colouring materials

Activity teaching notes:

- Warm-up: invite learners to mime the germination of a bean seed, starting curled up tightly, gradually opening, reaching upwards, with hands and arms, miming the leaves' development.
- Focus on the activity:

  1. Read out the task.
  2. Check that the task is understood.
  3. Ask for oral answers to the question about what sunflower seeds need to grow. Deal with any disagreements.
  4. The drawings should illustrate what learners think seeds need to grow. They can attempt a single picture including all these factors, or they can draw a small picture of each one separately.

- Follow-up – you could use these questions and additional activities.

Let everyone see the drawings produced by the class. Compare them and talk about differences.

Ideas for additional activities

Collate on the board a list of all the factors learners included in their drawings. Tally the numbers for each one and then total them. Ask learners to look at the totals and find the most common and the least common factor. If light and soil were in the list of factors you need to disagree with these ideas. Remind them of seed growing in *Workbook B* that did not have any soil. Ask learners to think about where seeds are normally put to start growing – underground. What is missing there?

Answers

- What drawn answers should include: the drawings should not include the sunlight or any other light and should show no soil. To grow, seeds must have water, air and warmth.

What seeds need

1 Look at the photo of seeds growing in soil.

2 What does a sunflower need to grow? Draw a sunflower and what you think it needs to grow.
   Show and tell.

18 Soil

UNIT 5 Buildings

Learning objectives

- To be able to identify and continue patterns
- To identify and name building types

Key words

building, wall, pattern, block

Topic introduction

- Name of topic: Buildings
- Things to talk about: have a class conversation about the variety of buildings learners have seen and gone into.

Buildings

Page 19

Materials needed:

- pencils, colouring materials, blocks of various colours

Activity teaching notes:

- Warm-up: look around the room to find patterns of any kind, including in clothes, curtains, carpets, walls, floors.

- Focus on the activity:

  1. Read out the task.
  2. Check that the task is understood.
  3. Each learner should complete the four patterns in the blank spaces below the incomplete patterns.
  4. The blocks should be used to make four different patterns, varying shapes and colours. Once their patterns are complete, learners draw them in the blank boxes.

- Follow-up – you could use these questions and additional activities.

The class should share the patterns they have made and compare them.

Ideas for additional activities

Select one pattern and get the learners to copy it using blocks.

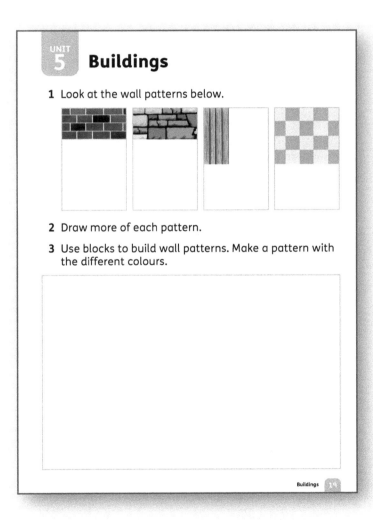

UNIT 5 Buildings

1 Look at the wall patterns below.

2 Draw more of each pattern.

3 Use blocks to build wall patterns. Make a pattern with the different colours.

Buildings 19

Answers

- Example answers:

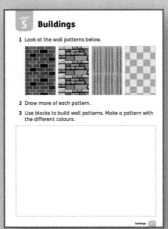

- What drawn answers should include: the incomplete patterns should be completed in the same colours and shapes as the printed pictures. The four patterns made by learners will be very varied.

Page 20

Materials needed:

- pencils, colouring materials

Activity teaching notes:

- Warm-up: ask learners about the different types of houses, particularly the materials that have been used in building them.
- Focus on the activity:
  1. Read out the task.
  2. Check that the task is understood.
  3. Remind the class to fill the space with a large drawing. Each learner is free to draw a house of any type.
- Follow-up – you could use these questions and additional activities.

Ask learners to show their house drawings. Compare them and sort them into sets on the basis of some criteria (e.g. number of windows, doors, shape of roof, building materials).

Ideas for additional activities

Invite learners to use blocks of various sizes and types (wood, plastic) to make a model building.

Answers

- What drawn answers should include: the drawings will all be different but should look like a house rather than any other type of building.

Page 21

Materials needed:

- pencils

Activity teaching notes:

- Warm-up: have a class conversation about buildings of different types and collate on the board the list of buildings mentioned by the class (e.g. shops, banks, offices, police stations, factories, apartment blocks).
- Focus on the activity:
  1. Read out the task.
  2. Check that the task is understood.
  3. Each learner draws lines from pictures to words.
- Follow-up – you could use these questions and additional activities.

Share the answers and ask how learners recognise the types of buildings.

Ideas for additional activities

Invite the class to compare the buildings in the pictures. Ask them to look for features that are common to all of them and features that are unique to each one.

Answers

- Example answers:

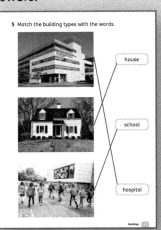

- What drawn answers should include: lines from pictures to words –hospital, house, school

5 Match the building types with the words.

house

school

hospital

Page 22

Materials needed:

- pencils, colouring materials

Activity teaching notes:

- Warm-up: encourage learners to imagine how buildings could be made differently in the future, using unusual materials and shapes. Let them share their ideas for changes.

- Focus on the activity:
  1. Read out the task.
  2. Check that the task is understood.
  3. Individuals are free to draw whatever they imagine future buildings could be. Remind the class to use the whole space provided.

- Follow-up – you could use these questions and additional activities.

Let learners see each other's drawings and discuss them. Learners can ask questions, compare their work and comment on it.

Ideas for additional activities

Make model buildings using scrap materials.

Answers

- What drawn answers should include: the buildings are meant to be unlike present-day buildings, so learners are free to express their imagination.

6 Draw your building of the future. Show and tell.

UNIT 6 Shops

Learning objectives

- To identify and name fruits and vegetables
- To sort containers into sets
- To sort and name seafoods
- To identify and name materials used to make furniture
- To describe and name textures

Key words

shop, fruit, vegetable, underline, count, favourite, circle, jar, set, can, tin, fish, shell, leg, furniture, feel, soft, rough, hard, smooth, fabric

Topic introduction

- Name of topic: Shops
- Things to talk about: have a class conversation about learners going shopping with their families.

Shops

Page 23

Materials needed:

- pencils, colouring materials

Activity teaching notes:

- Warm-up: ask learners to name fruits and vegetables and collate all the names on the board.
- Focus on the activity:
  1. Read out the task.
  2. Check that the task is understood.
  3. Learners should underline only the fruits in the word box.
  4. The numbers can then be added to the names.
  5. Learners are free to draw whatever fruit they choose.
- Follow-up – you could use these questions and additional activities.

Let learners see one another's fruit drawings and talk about them. Collate the names of the fruits on the board, total them and then ask learners to look at the data and comment on the fruits (e.g. most popular, least popular).

Ideas for additional activities

Ask learners to draw, colour and cut out a picture of their favourite fruit. Make a display of the drawings in the form of a pictogram, showing the size of each set.

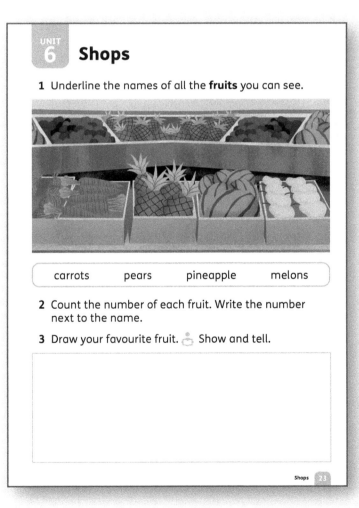

UNIT 6 **Shops**

1 Underline the names of all the **fruits** you can see.

| carrots | pears | pineapple | melons |

2 Count the number of each fruit. Write the number next to the name.

3 Draw your favourite fruit. Show and tell.

Shops 23

Food containers

Page 24

Materials needed:

- pencils

Activity teaching notes:

- Warm-up: have a class conversation about the ways food is packaged, listing learners' answers on the board (e.g. tins, jars, cardboard boxes, paper bags, plastic packets).
- Focus on the activity:
  1. Read out the task.
  2. Check that the task is understood.
  3. The counting and recording should be done after the items have been circled or crossed out.
- Follow-up – you could use these questions and additional activities.

Ask learners to report their answers to the class and deal with any disagreements.

Ideas for additional activities

Look around the classroom and identify the materials used in packaging classroom items (e.g. plastic pots, wooden boxes, paper, fabric bags).

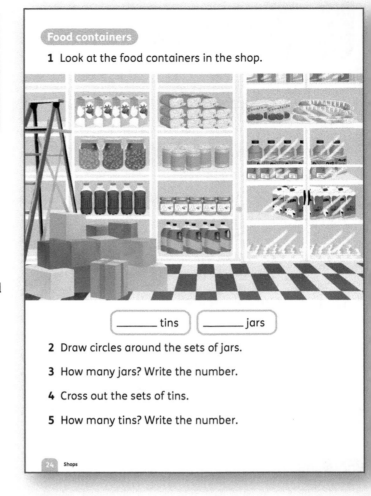

Food containers

1 Look at the food containers in the shop.

_____ tins   _____ jars

2 Draw circles around the sets of jars.

3 How many jars? Write the number.

4 Cross out the sets of tins.

5 How many tins? Write the number.

24 Shops

Fish

Page 25

Materials needed:

- pencils, colouring materials

Activity teaching notes:

- Warm-up: have a class conversation about fish and other seafood – learners' likes and dislikes.
- Focus on the activity:
  1. Read out the task.
  2. Check that the task is understood.
  3. Let learners talk to one another as they look at the picture.
  4. Each learner underlines the chosen words.
  5. Learners are free to draw any kind of fish. Remind them to use the whole space provided.
- Follow-up – you could use these questions and additional activities.

Ask learners to show their drawings and talk about them. Collate on the board the names of the fishes drawn and total them. Ask learners to identify the most common and least common fish drawings.

Ideas for additional activities

The class can make block graphs using the fish data, using interlocking cubes and/or large squared paper for learners to colour in the correct number of squares.

> ### Answers
> - Possible answers: underlined – crab, lobster, clam
> - What drawn answers should include: these will depend on learners' choices.

Furniture

Page 26

Materials needed:

- pencils

Activity teaching notes:

- Warm-up: allow learners to talk about furniture at home, with the focus on what items are made of and how they feel.

- Focus on the activity:

  1. Read out the task.

  2. Check that the task is understood.

  3. Have oral answers to the first question about what things in the picture feel like.

4. Each learner should write H on hard things, S on soft things, W on wooden things and F on things made of fabric.

- Follow-up – you could use these questions and additional activities.

Ask the class to share their answers and collate the four lists on the board. Ask learners to look at the data and discuss the differences (e.g. there are more wooden things than fabric, more hard things than soft.

Ideas for additional activities

Identify things in the classroom that are hard, soft, wooden or fabric then add other materials and textures to the list (e.g. metal, plastic, rough, smooth).

> ### Answers
> - Example answers:

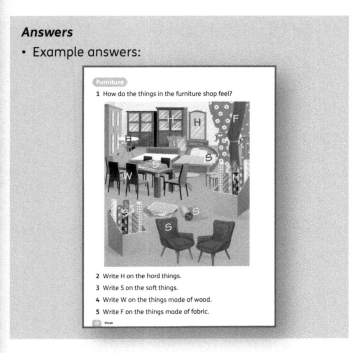

1 How do the things in the furniture shop feel?

2 Write H on the hard things.

3 Write S on the soft things.

4 Write W on the things made of wood.

5 Write F on the things made of fabric.

Learning objectives

- To sort and identify musical instruments on the basis of how they are played
- To identify animal, plant and non-living things
- To identify and name materials
- To be able to make a pot from clay

Key words

museum, hit, circle, blow, shake, pluck, beads, seeds, can, pot, stone, metal, wood, fabric, clay, pattern

Topic introduction

- Name of topic: Museums
- Things to talk about: let learners share their experiences of visiting museums.

Museums

Page 27

Materials needed:

- pencils, beads or seeds, pots or cans

Activity teaching notes:

- Warm-up: look at the musical instruments in the classroom and let learners compare how they are played.

- Focus on the activity:

  1. Read out the task.
  2. Check that the task is understood.
  3. Each learner should write H or S on things and circle or underline things shown in the picture.
  4. The shaker making can be done in pairs or groups, depending on the availability of the components.

- Follow-up – you could use these questions and additional activities.

Ask learners to play their shakers one at a time and then all together. Let them choose a favourite song and sing it with shaker accompaniment.

Ideas for additional activities

Invite learners to make other simple instruments for hitting and plucking (e.g. drums using empty pots or cans) with plastic or cling-film skins, cardboard or wooden boxes with elastic bands stretched over them. Let them play all the instruments together.

UNIT 7 Museums

1 Write H on the things you hit.
2 Circle those things you blow.
3 Write S on the things you shake.
4 Underline those things you pluck.

hit pluck shake blow

5 Make a shaker with beads or seeds and a pot or a tin.

Museums 27

Museum objects

Page 28

Materials needed:

- pencils, colouring materials, plasticine, playdough or modelling clay

Activity teaching notes:

- Warm-up: have a class conversation about stone and metal objects, with the focus on what their characteristics are. Find examples in the room and outside.

- Focus on the activity:

  1. Read out the task.

  2. Check that the task is understood.

  3. Each learner should find the stone things and put X on each one.

  4. Metal things should be circled.

  5. Let learners choose to draw or make a pot. Both forms should be decorated with a pattern.

- Follow-up – you could use these questions and additional activities.

Ask learners to show their drawings or model pots. Let the class compare and comment on them.

Ideas for additional activities

Suggest that learners use kitchen foil to make metal objects (e.g. coins, jewellery, spoons). Make a display of the pots and the metal objects.

Museum objects

1 Put ☒ on the stone things.

2 Circle the metal things.

3 Draw a pattern.

4 Draw a pot or make a pot. Add your pattern.
   Show and tell.

28 Museums

Page 29

Materials needed:

- pencils, fabrics, wood, metal foil, paints

Activity teaching notes:

- Warm-up: show the class pictures in books or online of famous paintings, murals, mosaics and ask for their reactions and opinions.

- Focus on the activity:

  1. Read out the task.

  2. Check that the task is understood.

  3. The blank space on the wall in the picture should be filled with a coloured drawing.

  4. Learners should be free to choose which material they use to make their gallery items.

- Follow-up – you could use these questions and additional activities.

Learners share their products and talk about them, answering questions from their peers.

Ideas for additional activities

Display all the objects made in the activity above and add to them over a period of time to create a 'class gallery'. Invite other classes to come and visit the gallery.

Answers

- What drawn answers should include: the drawings and the objects learners choose will vary. Anything chosen by learners will be acceptable as the museum shown contains a very general collection of items.

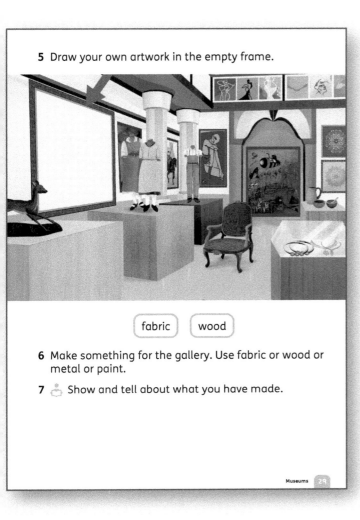

5 Draw your own artwork in the empty frame.

fabric   wood

6 Make something for the gallery. Use fabric or wood or metal or paint.

7 Show and tell about what you have made.

Museums 29

UNIT 8 In the street

Learning objectives

- To sort things on the basis of their movements or sounds
- To identify pushes and pulls and to use them

Key words

street, sort, set, engine, animal, person, moving, sounds, circle, number, cross out, machine, pull, push, wheels

Topic introduction

- Name of topic: In the street
- Things to talk about: have a class discussion about being in the street, sharing things that learners like and dislike.

In the street

Page 30

Materials needed:

- pencils

Activity teaching notes:

- Warm-up: collect a list of wheeled objects of all kinds, not just vehicles.
- Focus on the activity:
  1. Read out the task.
  2. Check that the task is understood.
  3. E is written on things that have an engine.
  4. Circles are drawn round the things with wheels but without an engine.
- Follow-up – you could use these questions and additional activities.

Let the class share their answers and deal with any differences in their answers. Talk about how things without engines can move. Focus on the forces of using the feet to push on pedals or the ground and the muscles of the horse moving its legs.

Ideas for additional activities

Invite learners to mime the different ways of moving shown in the picture then take them outside to play on the equipment with wheels.

UNIT 8 In the street

1 Write E on the things with an **engine**.

2 Circle the things with **wheels** that do **not** have an engine.

30 In the street

Answers

- Possible answers: **E** – car, truck, coach. **Circles –** bicycle, scooter

Example answers:

Sounds

Page 31

Materials needed:

- pencils

Activity teaching notes:

- Warm-up: ask the class to sit quietly and listen to sounds coming from inside and outside the school.

- Focus on the activity:

  1. Read out the task.

  2. Check that the task is understood.

  3. Each learner should circle the sound makers in the picture.

  4. As a class, listen to the sounds individual learners can make using different parts of their bodies. Share the circled items in the picture and deal with any disagreements.

- Follow-up – you could use these questions and additional activities.

Play a class game where one learner is 'leader' and the class follow in making the sounds chosen by the leader. Swap the leader role after each 'round' of the game.

Ideas for additional activities

Make cards with a source of sound on each one. Collect the words from the class (e.g. traffic, birds, people, dogs and other animals). Go outside with the cards, put them on the ground with a pot of beads or seeds to use as counters. Each time a sound is heard a learner puts a counter on the appropriate card. Back in class, count the counters for each type of sound and use the data to create a block graph from interlocking cubes and/or large squared paper. Have a class discussion about what the graph shows about sounds in the environment.

Answers

- Possible answers: circles – plane, birds, dog, baby, ambulance, drill car, people

- Example answers:

Sounds

1 Look for all the things making sounds. Draw circles around them. Count them.

2 Use your body to make 2 sounds.

3 Draw something that makes a sound.
 Show and tell.

In the street 31

Pull and push

Page 32

Materials needed:

- pencils

Activity teaching notes:

- Warm-up: ask learners to demonstrate pulling and pushing things

- Focus on the activity:

  1. Read out the task.

  2. Check that the task is understood.

  3. Learners should circle all the pulls in the picture, count them and record the number in the box.

  4. Learners should cross out all the pushes in the picture, count them and record the number in the box.

- Follow-up – you could use these questions and additional activities.

Let learners share their answers and deal with any disagreements.

Ideas for additional activities

Take the class outside and let them use equipment and toys such as hoops, balls and sand. Ask learners to identify whether they are pushing or pulling as they play.

Answers

- Possible answers: circles – suitcase on wheels: crossed out – pram, luggage trolley, cars

- Example answers:

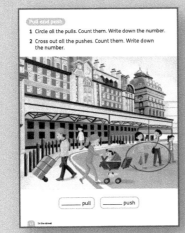

Pull and push

1 Circle all the pulls. Count them. Write down the number.

2 Cross out all the pushes. Count them. Write down the number.

_____ pull   _____ push

32   In the street

Page 33

Materials needed:

- pencils and colouring materials

Activity teaching notes:

- Warm-up: ask learners to push or pull large items in the room that do not have wheels and explain how it feels.

- Focus on the activity:

  1. Read out the task.

  2. Check that the task is understood.

  3. Remind learners to draw as large a picture as they can. They could add the words 'push' or 'pull' to the drawings.

- Follow-up – you could use these questions and additional activities.

Let learners share their drawings, compare them and comment on them.

Ideas for additional activities

Collate the types of toys on the board and total each type. Sort them into sets of pulled toys and pushed toys. Ask learners to talk about what the data shows (e.g. some toys can be pulled and pushed).

Answers

- What drawn answers should include: the toys must have wheels.

3 Draw a large toy with wheels. Can you pull it? Can you push it? Show and tell.

Learning objectives

- To be able to identify up and down
- To be able to slide things down a slope
- To arrange things in order of height
- To identify and name plant parts
- To make a bark wax rubbing
- To make shapes that roll
- To identify floating items
- To identify and name various forms of movement

Key words

park, up, down, slide, number, order, height, shorter, taller, tree, bark, leaf, bud, twig, wax, rubbing, lake, slope, roll, shape, float, tick, circle, movement, dough, plasticine

Topic introduction

- Name of topic: In the park

- Things to talk about: have a class discussion about visiting parks. Encourage learners to describe what they did there, particularly any kind of movement.

In the park

Page 34

Materials needed:

- pencils, large books (for slopes), objects to slide down slopes, colouring materials

Activity teaching notes:

- Warm-up: invite learners to use their hands and arms to mime 'up', 'down', 'moving up', 'coming down'.

- Focus on the activity:

1. Read out the task.

2. Check that the task is understood.

3. Learners write the words 'up' and 'down' to match where the children in the pictures are on each item of playground equipment.

- Follow-up – you could use these questions and additional activities.

Learners share their answers and talk about how they go from up to down, and from down to up in each case.

Ideas for additional activities

Take the class outside and let learners find places where they can go up and down in various ways.

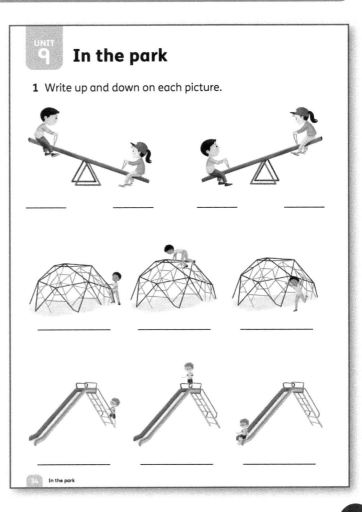

Page 35

Materials needed:

- pencils, colouring materials, large books, small items to slide down the books

Activity teaching notes:

- Warm-up: all learners hold a small non-round item on their flat hands and slowly tip them until the items slide off their hands. Repeat the action with different items.

- Focus on the activity:

  1. Read out the task.

  2. Check that the task is understood.

  3. The task is best done by pairs or groups of three. Let learners choose what to slide, using at least three different items each. Encourage them to talk as they explore what happens.

  4. Remind the class to fill all the available space with their drawings.

- Follow-up – you could use these questions and additional activities.

Let the class look at one another's drawings and describe what they show. Try to find out if learners found some items slid better or sooner than others and if so, why they think this happened (e.g. the material, the surface texture, the mass, the shape).

Ideas for additional activities

Go outside and test some of the learners' ideas about objects sliding.

Answers
- What drawn answers should include: each drawing will be for learners to choose so they will be very different, but a slope and sliding object/s must be included.

2 Use a big book to make a slide. Slide things down it.

3 Draw what you have done. Show and tell.

Trees

Page 36

Materials needed:

- pencils

Activity teaching notes:

- Warm-up: have a class conversation about trees to explore what learners already know and what they feel about trees.

- Focus on the activity:

  1. Read out the task.

  2. Check that the task is understood.

  3. Learners arrange the trees in order of height, writing 1 to 4 below or above them.

  4. The drawing of a shorter and a taller tree should be done in the space on the right.

  5. The tree parts should be linked by lines to the names in the boxes.

- Follow-up – you could use these questions and additional activities.

Let the class see the trees drawn by one another and compare the ordering of the tree pictures. Deal with any disagreements.

Ideas for additional activities

Take the class outside and encourage them to look at trees and touch the bark, leaves and buds. Let them use wax crayons and paper to make bark rubbings of different trees and compare the patterns that appear.

Answers

- Possible answers: order of trees – 1, 4, 3, 2.
- What drawn answers should include: the drawings should show a tree smaller than tree 1 and another taller than tree 4.

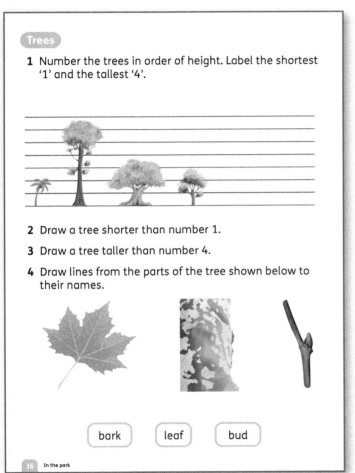

Trees

1 Number the trees in order of height. Label the shortest '1' and the tallest '4'.

2 Draw a tree shorter than number 1.

3 Draw a tree taller than number 4.

4 Draw lines from the parts of the tree shown below to their names.

bark   leaf   bud

Water

Page 37

Materials needed:

- Pencils, bowls, water, small objects to test in water

Activity teaching notes:

- Warm-up: have a class conversation about playing in water at bath time, in the sea, at the paddling or swimming pool.

- Focus on the activity:

1. Read out the task.

2. Check that the task is understood.

3. The floating things should be circled.

4. Animals that swim should be ticked.

5. Learners should be free to find small objects in the room that they want to test. The task should be done in groups and, if necessary, one by one group at a time. The items tested should be put into two sets – the floaters and the sinkers.

- Follow-up – you could use these questions and additional activities.

When all learners have tested their items and have made two sets, bring the class together to share their results. Collate the list of items in each set on the board and ask learners to compare them, coming to some form of conclusion if possible.

Ideas for additional activities

The testing of learners' ideas of why some things float and others do not could be further explored in the same way as above. They should learn that mass is not the key factor, which is a common misconception, especially in early years learners.

Answers

- Possible answers: circles – model boats, canoe, boats, birds, life-saving floats; swimming – ducks, fish

Water

1 Circle all the things that float.

2 Tick the things that swim.

3 Look for objects around the classroom. Find out whether they float using a bowl of water.

Movement

Page 38

Materials needed:

• pencils, modelling clay, large books or other slopes

Activity teaching notes:

• Warm-up: have a class discussion about the ways we can move using hands, feet, knees, etc.

• Focus on the activity:

   1. Read out the task.

   2. Check that the task is understood.

   3. Learners should circle all the moving things in the picture.

   4. Lines connecting the movements to the words in the boxes should be added.

   5. The modelling clay can be given to pairs or threes to make shapes that roll down the slopes of large books or other suitable surfaces in the room.

• Follow-up – you could use these questions and additional activities.

Let the class share their answers to the tasks on the page and deal with any disagreements. Let each pair/three show the shapes they made that can roll. Discuss what is common to all of them.

Ideas for additional activities

Take the class outside and encourage learners to move around in as many different ways as possible (e.g. walking, running, hopping, skipping, rolling on the grass).

Answers

• Possible answers: **Circles – Moving things** – kite, Frisbee, football, children running, children rolling.

Movement

1 Circle the moving things. Draw lines to the words.

| flying | rolling | running | resting |

| kicking | catching | throwing |

2 Use modelling clay to make two or more shapes that roll. Try them out on a slope.

38   In the park

UNIT 10 Staying safe

Learning objectives

- To identify and name safety features in the street and the classroom
- To identify and name sockets, switches and plugs
- To know that electricity is used by many appliances
- To identify and name dangers, including electricity and flames

Key words

safe, symbol, tick, count, crossing, match, traffic, lights, electricity, circle, socket, plug, number, flame, safety, dangerous, danger

Topic introduction

- Name of topic: Staying safe
- Things to talk about: have a class conversation about staying safe at home and in the street.

Staying safe

Page 39

Materials needed:

- pencils

Activity teaching notes:

- Warm-up: ask learners to name the dangers when walking in the street.
- Focus on the activity:
  1. Read out the task.
  2. Check that the task is understood.
  3. Learners identify the things that help to keep people safe and put ticks on them.
  4. The words are connected by lines to the symbols in the lights.
- Follow-up – you could use these questions and additional activities.

Collate the list of items learners ticked. Sort them into two or more sets, using criteria suggested by the learners (e.g. signs or symbols, people, equipment). Talk about the sets.

Ideas for additional activities

Take the class outside and ask them to role play being in the street, with some learners taking the adult roles, holding the hands of the 'children' in the role play. They should practise crossing the street, looking both ways for traffic and walking – not running – to the other side. Learners riding tricycles, scooters and toy cars could be included in the role play.

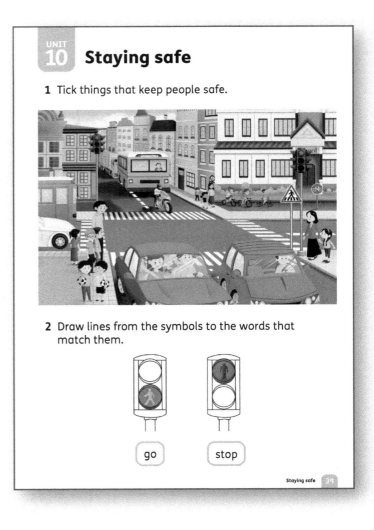

UNIT 10 Staying safe

1 Tick things that keep people safe.

2 Draw lines from the symbols to the words that match them.

go   stop

Staying safe 39

Answers

- Possible answers: pedestrian crossings and lights, traffic lights, road signs, helmets, seat belts, cycle lane, adults holding children's hands, balls being carried, pavements
- Example answers:

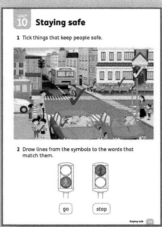

- What drawn answers should include: there should be lines from green man symbol to 'go' and red man symbol to 'stop'.

Electricity

Page 40

Materials needed:

- pencils, colouring materials

Activity teaching notes:

- Warm-up: ask learners what their parents and other adults have told them about being careful with electricity.
- Focus on the activity:
  1. Read out the task.
  2. Check that the task is understood.
  3. Learners mark everything electrical with a X.
  4. Circles should be drawn around sockets in the walls and lines drawn to the word 'socket'.
  5. The plugs not in sockets should be added up and the number written on the line.
- Follow-up – you could use these questions and additional activities.

Ask learners to name other things at home that use electricity. Collate the answers, including the items from the picture, on the board. Sort them into sets based on what the electricity is producing (e.g. movement, heat, sound).

Ideas for additional activities

Ask learners to move around the room and locate all the sockets. Keep a tally on the board of all the electrical items in the room. Sort them into the sets already made. Let learners work out what most items use electricity for.

Answers

- Possible answers: fan, radio, iron, fridge, toaster, kettle, cooker; sockets - 12

Fire

Page 41

Materials needed:

- pencils

Activity teaching notes:

- Warm-up: have a class conversation about fires, sharing the positive and negative features.
- Focus on the activity:
  1. Read out the task.
  2. Check that the task is understood.
  3. X should be added to all the flames.
  4. Words describing flames should be circled.
  5. The class should give oral answers to question **3**.

- Follow-up – you could use these questions and additional activities.

Let the class share their answers about flames. Move around the school with learners to locate the safety items shown in the pictures.

Ideas for additional activities
Take the class outside and invite them to role play fire-fighting, using any toy vehicles available to take the part of the fire engine. Ropes could be used as 'hoses' and the climbing frame or slide could become the ladder to rescue people high in the 'burning building'.

Answers
- Possible answers: flames – candle, match, wood fire, gas burner on cooker: circles – burn, hot, danger: safety items – this will vary from school to school, but all schools should have fire extinguishers, fire alarms and fire blankets.

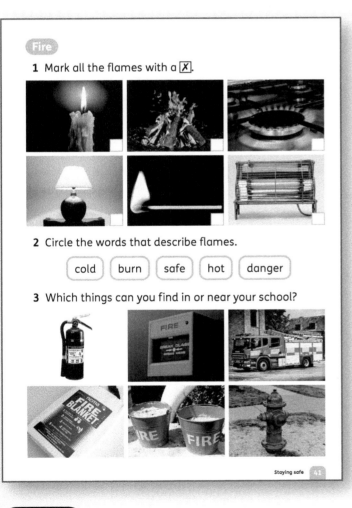

Danger
Page 42
Materials needed:
- pencils, colouring materials

Activity teaching notes:

- Warm-up: encourage learners to talk about things that they are afraid of.
- Focus on the activity:
  1. Read out the task.
  2. Check that the task is understood.
  3. Learners add an X to all the dangerous things shown on the page.
  4. Remind the class to fill the space with their drawing and let them choose freely what they draw.
- Follow-up – you could use these questions and additional activities.

Let learners share their answers about the dangerous things and deal with any disagreements. Ask learners to show their drawings to one another, ask questions and make comments.

Ideas for additional activities
List on the board the dangerous animals shown on the page. Ask learners to name other dangerous animals.

Answers
- Possible answers: X – scorpion, snake, spider, hot pan on gas burner, broken bottle, chemical liquid in bottle
- What drawn answers should include: the drawings will all be different as the dangerous things are chosen by learners.

Learning objectives

- To identify and name various forms of transport
- To mime transport movements

Key words

holiday, match, train, car, boat, plane, bus, tick, circle, mime, movement

Topic introduction

- Name of topic: Holidays

- Things to talk about: encourage learners to talk about their holiday experiences, particularly the ways they travelled and the activities they took part in.

Holidays

Page 43

Materials needed:

- pencils

Activity teaching notes:

- Warm-up: ask learners to mime travelling in various ways. One learner at a time could mime and the class be asked to identify the method of travel.

- Focus on the activity:

  1. Read out the task.

  2. Check that the task is understood.

  3. The five forms of transport should be linked with lines to the words in the boxes.

  4. Learners add ticks to the ones they have used.

  5. Circles are then added to favourites.

  6. Return to the warm-up task and ask learners to demonstrate the five types of transport for others to identify.

- Follow-up – you could use these questions and additional activities.

Ask learners for their favourite forms of transport. Collate the answers board; total each type. Create a block graph of the data using interlocking cubes and/or squared paper.

Ideas for additional activities

Take the class outside and invite them to enact the forms of transport shown in the pictures.

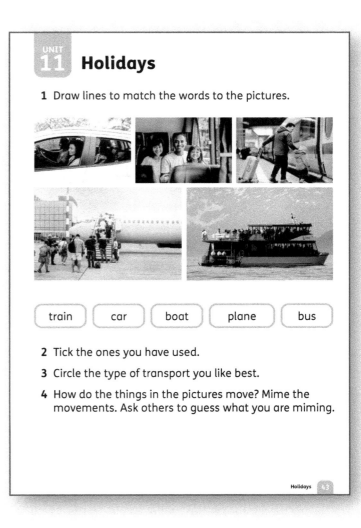

UNIT
11 Holidays

1 Draw lines to match the words to the pictures.

| train | car | boat | plane | bus |

2 Tick the ones you have used.

3 Circle the type of transport you like best.

4 How do the things in the pictures move? Mime the movements. Ask others to guess what you are miming.

Holidays 43

Answers

- Possible answers: the lines connect pictures to words – car, bus, train, plane, boat
- Example answers:

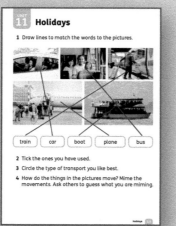

Holiday activities

Page 44

Materials needed:

- pencils

Activity teaching notes:

- Warm-up: have a class conversation about activities learners have done on holiday.
- Focus on the activity:
  1. Read out the task.
  2. Check that the task is understood.
  3. Learners add ticks to activities they enjoy.
  4. Lines should be drawn from the words to the pictures.
- Follow-up – you could use these questions and additional activities.

Ask learners to talk about the two activities not named on the page – the zoo and the aquarium. Focus on the way the different animals move.

Ideas for additional activities

Take the class outside and role play the animal movements talked about previously.

Answers

- Possible answers: the ticks will be put on things learners enjoy, so the answers will vary. Lines connecting words to pictures should link: ride to fairground; swim to pool; float to rowing boat; slide to skis.

Holiday activities

1 Tick the things you would like to do on holidays.
2 Match the words to the pictures. Draw lines.

float   slide   swim   ride

44   Holidays

Page 45

Materials needed:

- pencils, colouring materials

Activity teaching notes:

- Warm-up: ask learners to imagine going to places they have never been to (e.g. under the sea, in space, inside a deep cave).
- Focus on the activity:
  1. Read out the task.
  2. Check that the task has been understood.
  3. Remind the class to make their drawings fill all the space on the page.
- Follow-up – you could use these questions and additional activities.

Ask the learners to show their pictures to one another and talk about them.

Ideas for additional activities

Take the class outside and encourage them to enact some of the 'ideal' holiday ideas; dressing up if possible and using play equipment for transport, etc.

Answers

- What drawn answers should include: learners are free to choose their ideal holiday so the drawings will vary. There will be imaginative responses to the task along with some degree of realism.

3 Draw your ideal holiday.  Show and tell.

Holidays 45

Glossary

adult – adults are fully grown animals and people

age – your age is the numbers of years you have lived

animals – living things that must eat plants or other animals as food

birds – animals that have feathers and lay eggs on land

burn – when an object burns it gives off heat. Flames rise from burning things

colours – there are millions of colours. We can see colours, but some animals only see in black and white

complete – to finish; to fill in

describe – use words to tell what something is like

egg – the starting point for a new animal

electricity – electricity is a flow of energy. It usually comes from a battery or from the mains

engine – engines are machines that can move things. Engines need fuel such as petrol, diesel or coal to work

fish – scaly animals without legs; they lay eggs in water

flame – flames are produced when a fire is burning

float – objects float in water when they are not resting on the bottom

flower – the part of the plant that can produce a fruit

food – animals need food for energy and to help them grow. Plants make their own food from water, air and sunlight

fruit – the part of the plant that has seeds in it

group – a set of things with something in common

grow – living things grow and get larger

hard – an object that cannot easily be cut or squashed is hard

healthy – making the body strong and well

leaf/leaves – plants make food in their leaves

Moon – the Moon is a rocky ball that goes round the Earth. Other planets have moons going round them, too

pattern – when something is repeated

plants – green living things that make food using sunlight, water and a gas from the air

pull – a force that moves an object towards the source of the force

push – a force that moves an object away from the source of the force

root – the part of the plant that takes water from the soil

season – a time each year when the weather is different from before or after

seeds – the parts of a plant made in fruits and which can grow into new plants

shell – shells are the hard outer coverings of snails and some sea animals

soil – soil is a mixture of ground-up rock and the remains of dead plants and animals

soft – easily squashed, bent or shaped

sound – sound is caused by vibrations. You hear sound with your ears

stars – stars are suns that are so far away they look like tiny points of light in the night sky

type – a kind of; a sort of something

water – a liquid that is essential for all living things